Misplaced Blame

Misplaced Blame

Decades of Failing Schools, Their Children, and Their Teachers

Bonnie Johnson

ROWMAN & LITTLEFIELD
Lanham • Boulder • New York • London

Published by Rowman & Littlefield
An imprint of The Rowman & Littlefield Publishing Group, Inc.
4501 Forbes Boulevard, Suite 200, Lanham, Maryland 20706
www.rowman.com

6 Tinworth Street, London SE11 5AL, United Kingdom

Copyright © 2021 by Bonnie Johnson

All rights reserved. No part of this book may be reproduced in any form or by any electronic or mechanical means, including information storage and retrieval systems, without written permission from the publisher, except by a reviewer who may quote passages in a review.

British Library Cataloguing in Publication Information Available

Library of Congress Cataloging-in-Publication Data

Names: Johnson, Bonnie, 1948– author.
Title: Misplaced blame : decades of failing schools, their children, and their teachers / Bonnie Johnson.
Description: Lanham, Maryland: Rowman & Littlefield, 2021. | Includes bibliographical references and index. | Summary: "Misplaced Blame: Decades of Failing Schools, Their Children and Their Teachers examines the underlying causes of why schools fail"—Provided by publisher.
Identifiers: LCCN 2021019978 (print) | LCCN 2021019979 (ebook) | ISBN 9781475852288 (cloth) | ISBN 9781475852295 (paperback) | ISBN 9781475852301 (epub)
Subjects: LCSH: Public schools—United States—Evaluation. | Public schools—United States—Finance. | Educational tests and measurements—United States. | Educational accountability—United States.
Classification: LCC LA217.2 .J639 2021 (print) | LCC LA217.2 (ebook) | DDC 370.973—dc23
LC record available at https://lccn.loc.gov/2021019978
LC ebook record available at https://lccn.loc.gov/2021019979

For Dale

Contents

Foreword		vii
Preface		xi
Acknowledgments		xiii
Introduction		1
1	Failing Schools	3
2	The Realities of an Underfunded School: August, September	15
3	Regulating Teaching: October	35
4	Drugs, Poverty, and Test Scores: November, December	49
5	Test Preparation, the Pace Quickens: January, February	61
6	"The People in Washington Should See This School": March, April	77
7	The End of a School Year and Recommendations for Policy Change	93
8	The Changing Roles of Teachers	107
9	Some Costs of Poverty and Glimmers of Hope	135
Bibliography		145
Index		151
About the Author		155

Foreword

"We have met the enemy and he is us."—Walt Kelly, Pogo Comic Strip, Okefenokee Swamp, 1971

"We could wash dogs to get money for a screen."—Randall, third-grade pupil, Redbud Elementary

WE ARE FAILING *OUR* SCHOOLS

If you have had a teacher play a role in your life, you should read this book. This work is a wake-up call for anyone who cares about the most valuable assets that we have in this country—the minds and creativity of our children. It is difficult to comprehend how much talent is left behind and lost forever because we are failing our schools.

Dr. Bonnie Johnson and I are sister and brother; we traveled divergent paths to reach our current stations. We were fortunate to have a mother who read to us daily. She often worked outside the home, so this must not have been easy; the five of us were not always in adorable mode. Our father, who began his work in the trades, earned his teaching certificate and taught in the criminal justice system for many years.

Our formal education began in a two-room country schoolhouse and continued in a small-town public school system. In both locales, our teachers were admired, appreciated, and respected by community members. After teaching in public schools for many years, Bonnie went on to university teaching, and I went on to practice medicine—oncology—with an emphasis on teaching others in the medical profession. I believe in the motto "Do a good job teaching the next generation, because they are the ones who will take care of you." Teaching is in our blood, and our enthusiasm for the profession has been passed down to my two daughters, Jane and Carol, who are educators.

Dr. Johnson, with her late husband, Dr. Dale D. Johnson (who was a professor and chair of curriculum and instruction at the University of Wisconsin–Madison and led the Wisconsin Center for Education Research), decided one day to step away from their successful careers in academia to join the front lines in teaching full-time in an impoverished (resource-wise—not talent-wise) public school. They taught third and fourth grades. What follows this foreword is a poignant telling of how bad it is "out there," and what we need to do about it.

If you care anything about the next generation, this book will be unsettling. How can we see so much talent, creativity, and drive go to waste? You will be taken into the classrooms of Redbud Elementary School, where we will be introduced to the children who show so much promise. When confronted with no projector screen in their roach/spider-infested school in a dangerous neighborhood, one boy, for example, suggested washing dogs to make the money to buy a screen. Other children pondered that perhaps if they lived close to the president in Washington, they could get more money for their school (out of the mouths of babes). As I read that, I immediately said to myself that I would like to hire those kids—they are problem-solvers! As you read about these children in their formative years, and then see things go off track for them, you have to ask yourself, *Where did we fail them?*

With days upon days of challenges the children face—a broken neighborhood, dirty classrooms, no school supplies, poverty, drugs—we see our teachers begin to be broken by "the system" of standardized test scores. We see that for each little student, passing a single year-end test consumes their lives. It is sink or swim with no tutors to assist those who need extra help. Eventually a child breaks, and all is lost; it is sickening.

We are asked how we can teach everyone in the same manner when economically privileged students, for example, think that food stamps are stickers put on apples and bananas to identify the country of origin. Prior knowledge varies from individual to individual, and if a child does not possess requisite prior knowledge for school tasks, we must build it—not punish the child for not having it.

Dr. Johnson does not leave us with only problems. She offers sound, concrete, level-headed ways to correct the situation, including ways to secure more volunteers and ways to help fund local schools. Foremost of those recommendations is doing away with high-stakes standardized tests as the only way to judge a student's readiness for promotion or graduation. We should not rob teachers of their professional judgment. Teachers should not be scapegoats for addressing education's shortcomings.

Finally, we are reminded that we can save the rich, creative minds of our children. Being a cancer doctor, because of the importance of cancer research, I have seen many breakthroughs against the disease that have saved many patients' lives. We can do the same for the creative minds of our children.

As the adults in the room, we need to do everything that we can to make certain that children have enough to eat (without lunch-shaming them), and that they have a secure, clean learning environment with adequate teaching and learning supplies. Given those things, the teachers and the children will know what to do. Among other things, they will learn how to "tinker" to create new science, new art, new machines, and new real (not artificial) intelligence. We need to adapt Pogo's words to, "We have met the enemies and they aren't our teachers and schools." This book and its teachings are a call to *our* actions.

Daniel D. Von Hoff, MD, FACP, FASCO,
FAACR; Distinguished Professor,
Translational Genomics Research Institute
and City of Hope;
Professor of Medicine, Mayo Clinic,
Scottsdale, Arizona
2021

Preface

The Honorable John R. Lewis stated, "When you see something that is not right, not just, not fair, you have a moral obligation to say something." This volume is one educator's effort to meet that obligation.

It has been 20 years since Dale D. Johnson and I took leaves-of-absence from our university faculty and administrative positions to return, full-time, to public school classroom teaching. Much has changed during that time: the untimely death of Dr. Dale Johnson, the fourth-grade teacher in the pages that follow; the ballooning of the standards and accountability movement; the belittlement of teachers, who as the effects of the COVID-19 virus illustrated, are indispensable parts of our national fabric; and the public humiliation of schools that serve the economically poor.

An examination of why schools fail is necessary because the accountability spotlight usually focuses on the students, teachers, and administrators who learn and work in these environments. Blame is routinely placed on school personnel rather than on the systems in which they must function.

The correlation between family income and test scores is indisputable. Labels, school letter grades, and number of stars reflect a lack of student opportunities—nothing more. As long as failing schools depend on local and state tax dollars for large chunks of their operating budgets, and as long as fear is a tactic used to raise test scores, one cannot expect changes in anything. There have been attempts, through statistical formulae, to account for the effects of poverty on student achievement, but regardless of the noble intentions behind such endeavors, mere numbers do not relate what students and their teachers encounter every school day.

The events within several of the following chapters took place in an underfunded school as the accountability movement, with its emphasis on standardized test scores, began. It serves as a critical ethnography that shows who holds the power in an underfunded school. It is hoped that the lessons contained in this record will be used to initiate discussions for change—change that might lessen the chipping away at human potential.

The precise location of Redbud Elementary School is not important; what happened within its walls could happen in any school district where family income is low, the buildings are in disrepair, there are no dollars for "extras" such as art or music or tutoring, and test scores are the driving factor in determining the efficacy of teaching and learning.

The story of Redbud Elementary is one that should have had a sunnier, more hopeful revisit. There often are opportunities for second chances, but what we have lost in 20 years as a nation cannot be replaced.

Acknowledgments

To emphasize the multidisciplinary importance of this book's content, I moved outside the field familiar to me, education, to seek a foreword writer. I was fortunate to enlist Daniel D. Von Hoff, MD, an eminent oncologist. He is a distinguished professor at the Translational Genomics Research Institute and at City of Hope and is a professor of medicine at the Mayo Clinic. Dr. Von Hoff has served as the president of the American Association for Cancer Research and is a fellow of the American College of Physicians. When those outside the realm of education add their voices in recognizing the injustices of underfunded schools as Dr. Von Hoff has, perhaps the belittlement of these schools will be replaced with economic essentials that schools in well-off districts take for granted.

An author could not ask for a more knowledgeable and attentive publishing trio than Dr. Thomas Koerner, vice president and senior executive editor, Rowman & Littlefield; Ms. Carlie Wall, managing editor, Rowman & Littlefield; and Ms. Catherine Herman, production editor, Rowman & Littlefield. Thank you for your support throughout the project.

My gratitude to Dr. Yvonne Pratt-Johnson, who, among many other kind deeds, spared me from becoming a regular on the late-night Q30/Q31 back to Manhattan. I also acknowledge Dr. Mary Beth Schaefer and Molly; their compassion for others is an inspiration.

Introduction

"Failing Schools," Chapter 1 of this volume, begins with some arrest records of former pupils of a failing school, Redbud Elementary. The school and the town where it is located are described as they were 20 years ago and as they remain today. The branding of underfunded schools as "failing," some motives behind the label, and media coverage of failing schools are discussed. Unreasonable expectations for all public schools and their teachers are addressed, as are the conditions—lack of repairs and appropriate supplies—in failing schools. The chapter concludes with the relentless and short-sighted comparisons of American public schools with those in other countries.

Chapter 2, "The Realities of an Underfunded School: August, September," begins the story of a failing school at the dawn of the accountability movement two decades ago. It is told as the school days were lived; therefore, it is in narrative form and uses personal pronouns. Comments of teachers and their students, voices not often heard by those who mandate school policies, are prominent. Chapter 2 describes the dismal conditions of Redbud Elementary and several school regulations. The waste of instructional time on numerous assessments is highlighted. The chapter, and the five that follow in the chronology of a school year, contain excerpts from *High Stakes: Poverty, Testing and Failure in American Schools*, second edition (Rowman & Littlefield, 2006).

In Chapter 3, "Regulating Teaching: October," a costly test-prep computer program exemplifies how funds in a failing school are allocated. Parent-teacher conferences, daily demands on teachers and accompanying busywork, and students' knowledge of drugs are recounted. Solutions to a lack of classroom supplies are provided by pupils.

A book fair where students cannot afford to buy books, a mother who every day is "drunk or gone," students' lack of prior vocabulary knowledge used in school-related materials, a break-in at Redbud Elementary, and lack of heat in classrooms are among the topics reported in Chapter 4, "Drugs, Poverty, and Test Scores: November, December."

"Test Preparation, the Pace Quickens: January, February," Chapter 5, includes news of a murder near the school, test-prep pep rallies, and classroom rodent problems amid test-preparation frenzy. A school of academic distinction is featured on a local television station.

In Chapter 6, "'The People in Washington Should See This School': March, April," logistics for standardized test administration, field-testing future standardized tests, threats of a "bad label" for Redbud Elementary, and comments by visitors to the school are described.

Test performances and demographics and informing pupils that they have "failed" are components of Chapter 7, "The End of a School Year and Recommendations for Policy Change." Suggestions for policy changes that would lead to real education reform are discussed.

"The Changing Roles of Teachers" are described in Chapter 8. Historical notes that include the treatment of teachers throughout the years and curricular changes are described, and the impact of state and federal policies on what transpires in classrooms are examined. Factors that contribute to a teacher shortage, mandates for teacher educators, and the impact of changes on the nation's competitive future are highlighted.

In Chapter 9, "Some Costs of Poverty and Glimmers of Hope," the effects of hunger on schoolchildren, the ramifications of job losses on families, and the unsafe neighborhoods where children see disturbing events are discussed. Programs that serve as models for improving students' lives are described. The programs are founded and supported by those who know best how to solve problems in education—our teachers.

Chapter One

Failing Schools

THE CHILDREN AND THEIR TOWN

Attempted murder—sentence: 30 years of hard labor. Arrest for second-degree battery—bond set at $15,000. Possession of a concealed weapon by a convicted felon. Arrest for drug possession and sales. Two counts of aggravated burglary—bond set at $20,000. These are some of the offenses committed by those who, as children, attended a failing school. Among those arrested are repeat offenders, but others are not. Two of the children who attended the school are deceased; as young adults, they were murdered on different days in the neighborhood not far from where the failing school, Redbud Elementary,[1] still stands.

The perpetrators above were students in a third- and a fourth-grade class at Redbud Elementary 20 years ago; none of those children showed signs of trouble. They most often were kind to each other in the ways of children; they wanted to learn, and they were eager to please their teachers. Some would put complimentary handwritten notes and drawings on their teachers' desks.

Stickers and small plastic animals, won for commendable work in short sessions with a literacy coach/reading specialist, were given to the homeroom teachers as small gifts. One child—now in prison until he is 54 years old—found an old heart paperweight somewhere and gave it to his teacher for Valentine's Day. Toward the end of the school year, one of the third-graders, now a prisoner in his early 30s, had some difficulty paying attention in class and started to hoard items in his lift-top school desk. These behaviors occurred after the child's grandmother was murdered close to the school.

The town where the failing school is located looks about the same as it did 20 years ago—almost half of the buildings are empty, and many need extensive repairs. Industries that were mainstays have come and gone. A grant of $25,000 recently was awarded to the town to create a center where local artists can sell their works, but art purchases—even if the prices are nominal—require dollars that must be spent on essentials rather than on soul-lifting pieces of art.

Community leaders, trying to improve economics in the town, are intrepid and deserve plaudits, but to lure industry and good-paying jobs, it will take more than admirable intentions. It will take a well-educated workforce and an attractive community where people want to work and play. As in other small towns, the challenge is overwhelming without assistance from state or federal funds.

THE SCHOOL

Redbud Elementary, the only public school in the town, continues to be shamed through annual state "report cards." Grades on these report cards range from a D to an F. It is possible that the variance in these low grades is due to the "achievement," as measured by standardized tests, of the groups of children who take the tests in a given year.

No teacher or administrator who worked at Redbud Elementary remains 20 years later. This is not remarkable—two decades have passed; however, many of adults left after only a few years at the school. Several teachers who did not retire went to school districts where things were easier. The children did not and do not have this choice.

In the past 20 years, Redbud Elementary students have written competitive test-prep cheers, have listened to local speakers and a hired "motivational" speaker to get them "ready" for tests, and have seen classmates vie for monetary prizes ($3,750 divided among all third- through twelfth-grade students who achieved Advanced and Mastery levels on standardized tests).[2] Test-taking tips have appeared in local newspapers; one carried the following advice from a guidance counselor in the state:

- Make sure that your child has a good night's sleep the night before, and a good breakfast the morning of the test (I've been told that blueberries are "brain" food—but haven't actually seen the research).
- Reduce stress levels in the home by providing a relaxed environment—perhaps by playing classical music, such as Mozart, Bach, or Vivaldi, and refraining from arguments.[3]

The counselor apparently had not been to Redbud Elementary, where children who ate free breakfasts at school had no say in fruit selection, nor had the counselor witnessed the dangerous Redbud neighborhood after dark, where Vivaldi concertos and Bach fugues did not waft from dwellings.

BRANDING SCHOOLS AS "FAILING"

The derisive terms *failing school*, *troubled school*, and *struggling school* reflect an unawareness or dismissal of the factors that contribute to below-average standardized test scores, poor student attendance, low graduation rates, and other factors that can be numerically represented. Investigators would be hard-pressed to name many failing schools that do not enroll students mainly from low-income families. These schools usually have low teacher salaries due to a meager local tax base, buildings that need repairs, a shortage of specialists such as literacy coaches, lack of art or music classes, and more.

If those who blame the schools understand that there are circumstances beyond teachers' control that might contribute to below-average test scores but they refuse to acknowledge these circumstances, then the blamers are instigators and perpetuators of one of the biggest bamboozlements in the history of American education.

Some might argue that a more sinister effort, modeled on the Lancasterian system of the early 1800s, which used drill as its primary pedagogy, is behind the aims to shame public schools. Katz wrote:

> As a result of such schooling, the working class would be alert, obedient, and so thoroughly attuned to discipline through group sanctions that a minimum of policing would ensure the reservation of social order. But, and this is important, programmed from an early age to compete with one another, working-class children would not grow up to form a cohesive and threatening class force.[4]

If one set out to make certain that students, their teachers, and their schools would be labeled as failing, then one would institute "rigorous" demands in terms of standards and testing, not fund efforts to meet these demands, send the students to schools that lacked materials and a setting conducive to learning, let pupils go without adequate meals and medical care, place them in unsafe neighborhoods, pay their teachers chicken feed, and then voilà, failing schools such as Redbud Elementary would be replicated nationwide. This is what has happened.

Schools in the past have had reputations for being "tough" because of disrespectful, hard-nosed students in dangerous neighborhoods whose undaunted teachers led their students to the shining lights of knowledge and love of learning. Hollywood has made money on portrayals of rough schools in films such as *Stand and Deliver* and *Freedom Writers*. There are such heroic teachers at all grade levels in today's failing schools, but instead of having movies made about them, they are humiliated through newspaper headlines and television spots that announce their D or F state report cards.

WHY DID PEOPLE BUY INTO THE NOTION OF FAILING SCHOOLS?

British linguist J. R. Firth said, "You shall know a word by the company it keeps." Some words keep company in fixed order such as *fast food*, *hermetically sealed*, and *torrential downpour*. These word pairs occur frequently enough that linguists refer to them as *word freezes*. The word pair *public schools* has been keeping shady company since the era of school accountability mandates; it is now a part of the word freeze *failing public schools*.

It is apparent why those who have something to gain financially, or those who support a certain political ideology, persistently refer to *failing public schools*. It is not immediately apparent why the general public has bought into such a notion, but business principles of marketing supply some answers. The "newer is better" premise is a pillar of sales. Whether hawking laundry detergent, cereal, or malware detectors, marketing personnel rely on human tendencies to think that something new is more efficient, more thoroughly researched, or more innovative than something old.

Public schools are old; they were established in the 1830s. Their structure remains static: school board, superintendent, teachers, and costs mainly funded by local taxes. Newer instructional delivery models must be better: private schools charge tuition, and as the adage goes, you get what you pay for. This ignores the many accomplished Americans who attended public schools. Nobel Prize recipients in chemistry, and physiology or medicine, for example, speak highly of their public-school backgrounds (see chapter 8).

Those who gain financially, politically, or ideologically from dubbing public schools as failing must find a *competitor analysis* of the schools a breeze. The marketing term *competitor analysis* means "the process of identifying key competitors; assessing their objectives, strategies, strengths and weaknesses, and reaction patterns; and selecting which competitors to attack or avoid."[5]

Until the publication of *A Nation at Risk*[6] in 1983, there were not many public school competitors except for elite private schools and religious schools. Objectives of the public schools were determined by states or local school districts. Strengths included accepting all students; weaknesses included education funded mostly by local tax dollars. Attack modes were not difficult to determine because the public schools had no resources in place to combat these attacks—no one to tout their accomplishments, no powerful, connected personnel to justify their needs.

Denouncing public schools as failing has been a type of *brand positioning*,[7] a marketing term that addresses not only institutions and products but also the minds of consumers. Ries and Trout wrote, "Positioning starts with a product. A piece of merchandise, a service, an institution, or even a person. But positioning is not what you do to a product. Positioning is what you do to the mind of the prospect."[8]

Some media outlets have been helpful in the disparagement of public schools. The criticism might be unwitting and considered just a reporter's job; however, newspaper headlines and television spots that tap tap tap into readers' minds with news of failing schools are bound to affect consumer attitudes. A few examples are below.

"76 Alabama Schools on 'Failing' List"[9]
"Failing Grades for Many WV Public Schools"[10]
"Rockford Public Schools Get Failing Grade From the State of Illinois"[11]
"Public Schools Get Failing Grades in New Survey by Fort Lauderdale Residents"[12]
"Multiple Austin-Area Schools Earn Failing Grades From Texas Education Agency"[13]
"See If California Has Identified Your School as Low-Performing"[14]
"Report Cards Are Out for Ohio Schools and 309 Failed"[15]

The following headlines could be written about the failing school and its families described in the chapters that follow:

"Rodents Repeatedly Chew Through Classroom Computer Cables"
"Father Attempts to Burn Down Family Home"
"Third-Grader's Mother Jailed for Fighting"
"Child Returns to Classroom; Has Now Attended 5 Schools in 3 Months"
"Second Coldest Winter Since 1895—Some Classrooms Without Heat"
"Mother of Redbud Pupil 'Is in the Pen for Drugs'"
"Third Grader: 'My Real Dad Choked and Kicked My Mama'"
"Redbud Family Living in Pop-Up Trailer: No Running Water, No Electricity"

Various descriptors are used to identify failing schools (e.g., "27 SF [i.e., San Francisco] Unified Schools 'Low Performing,' Need Improvement, State Says: Nine Are Among the Worst in the State"[16]). Stars, report cards with grades from A to F, dashboards, and scorecards are among the reporting systems used to name schools that do not "measure up" to goals set by individual states. *Struggling* seems to be a descriptor in vogue at this writing (e.g., "State: 341 Iowa Schools Are Struggling and Need Comprehensive or Targeted Improvements"[17]).

As the saying goes, "Statistics represent faces with the tears wiped off,"[18] and numbers of students who have not met expectations do not tell the stories behind quantifiable data. There are formulae for softening these data by factoring in numbers of pupils on free lunch, for example; however, despite probable good intentions of those who devise such formulae, no fiddling with numbers can represent hungry children, haunted by violent acts witnessed in their neighborhoods, in the way that seeing these children every school day can.

UNREASONABLE EXPECTATIONS FOR PUBLIC SCHOOLS AND THEIR TEACHERS

Public schools have become temporary and more long-lasting repositories for the whims of influential folks and for those pushing political platforms designed to please constituents. Whether it is adopting sets of standards, increasing STEM (i.e., Science, Technology, Engineering, Mathematics) curricular offerings over the liberal arts, or getting "tougher" by "raising the bar" on teachers and their students, those with money and power generally set the rules.

In reviewing school board membership across 610 school districts in Ohio, for example, Bartanen and colleagues[19] found that school board members within neighborhoods of school districts had more money, were better educated, and were Whiter. This could mean that non-White low-income students' needs are more easily overlooked in some districts. In addition, running for any office takes time and often dollars; those who work long hours at low-paying jobs do not have an excess of either.

Public schools take all children into their classrooms. The nation expects much of these institutions—everything from teaching table manners and taking turns to the youngest to advanced algebra and the value of a well-turned phrase to the oldest. Just teaching most children how to read is an impressive intellectual endeavor: *thorough, through*; *heat, great*; *nose, lose*; *might, mite*; *to, too, two*; *plane, plain*; *chilly, chili*—six pronunciation challenges and four sets of homophones among millions of words.

There are multiple meanings for words that must be taught: The computer is *down*. Water *down* the soup. The Packers made a first *down*. Australia: *Down* Under. He scrubbed *down* the railings. She brought *down* the house with her jokes. Buckle *down*. Put your foot *down*. Just simmer *down*, and at least 81 other uses of *down*.[20]

Health issues and safety issues are expected to be addressed within school walls. Skolnick and Currie[21] pointed out decades ago, before the standards and accountability movement gained strength, that it is convenient if problems can be blamed on the schools, because then people do not have to worry about "nutrition, health and day care, decent housing, or the children's issues in general." Skolnick and Currie wrote:

> It's hard to know how much . . . can be controlled by the school and how much comes from our indifferent intellectual atmosphere. Given the enormous changes in the demographics of American schools and considering the idiot culture in which our students live most of the day, it's surprising the schools have done as well as they have.[22]

Now that schools are held accountable for low test scores, poor attendance, and low graduation rates, groups such as politicians, policymakers, and public-school critics can further avoid responsibility for complex societal ills such as poverty and racism. Those who grew up economically poor might say that they worked their way to an education and a more prosperous life; they went to schools without frills, so why can't others?

These reminiscences veil the complexities of contemporary poverty and schooling, such as absent parents or guardians who are working more than one minimum-wage job, lack of experienced teachers and community support, and harsh testing mandates that discourage students in underfunded schools.

There are simplistic notions that changing school personnel or instituting state "takeovers" will remedy low test scores and raise attendance and graduation rates. Where are the fairy godmothers, under monikers such as "improvement coaches" and "capacity builders,"[23] who will do this work? Chatter about bringing the "best teachers" into failing schools is laughable. Who wants to commute into dangerous neighborhoods to spend hours on writing "improvement plans" in demoralizing buildings only to be disparaged for not being "successful"?

Even when enticing bonuses are offered to teachers to move to failing schools in nearby geographic areas, the teachers won't budge.[24] They know that improvement plans and takeovers are doomed without changes in students' nutrition, medical care, and home lives; money for school materials and building repairs; and neighborhood safety.

INSUFFICIENT FUNDING OF BUILDINGS AND SUPPLIES

Sedgwick[25] gathered submissions from teachers who described the buildings in which they teach. Among the descriptions were ceilings with holes and leaks (one ceiling housing wasps), walls in need of paint, a building from 1938 lacking renovation, 25 students in a hotel-room-size classroom, and leaking windows.

Teachers also described old sets of textbooks with not enough of them for students to take home, nonworking computers, an art teacher making watercolors by soaking markers, broken desks, and a shortage of basic supplies such as tape. All the teaches reported spending their own money so that their students could have enough of what well-funded schools take for granted.

Truong[26] described Virginia schools that had rodent problems, leaky roofs, falling ceiling tiles, unreliable heating and cooling systems, mold; a superintendent reported the situation in his district as "borderline criminal." Heating problems caused some students to wear coats and other cold-weather gear as they sat in their cold January/February Baltimore, Maryland,[27] and Jackson, Mississippi,[28] classrooms.

Hall reported that a Wisconsin high school needed "a lot of money to bring it up to code," citing "major repairs" to electrical and plumbing systems.[29] A parent in Oklahoma stated that a school in her district was using 10-year-old science textbooks that did not support curriculum standards; a teacher in that state described building a usable desk from parts of broken desks.[30]

Who will supply the funds for needed up-to-date instructional materials and building repairs? Local school districts, unless they have well-off residents, already pinch pennies, states have other financial obligations—such as fixing roads—and the federal government, with its No Child Left Behind, Race to the Top, and the Every Student Succeeds Act, has expected performance for money.

Those who bemoan the money already spent on education rarely look at where those dollars land. Do they go to test-prep materials? Are they used for "consultants" who promise to raise test scores? Or is the money given directly to classroom teachers for age-appropriate supplies that they know will support their students' learning?

Cohen reported that Franklin D. Roosevelt allocated more than $1 billion for building and repairing public schools—and this followed the Great Depression (1929–1933). One of the budget-cutting calamities of the Great Recession (circa 2007–2009) was funding at all levels for school infrastructure. No one has emulated Roosevelt's allocation. Cohen also referred to a report card grade of D+ given to public schools by the American Society of Civil Engineers—not because of test scores but because of the rundown buildings.[31]

In Policy Statement 452—Investing in America's Schools—the American Society of Civil Engineers, a group comprised of those who design and build roads, bridges, airports, and other infrastructure components, wrote:

> The federal government has not assessed the condition of America's schools since 1999, when it estimated that $127 billion was needed to bring facilities into a good condition. . . . Quality education, obtained in a safe environment, is essential for the continued competitiveness and viability of our nation. The neglect of public school buildings and their ability to support education programs erodes [the American] our society's ability to compete in a global market.[32]

The society estimated the amount to "modernize and maintain" America's schools now is a minimum of $380 billion.

A Congressional Bill, H.R. 865—Rebuild America' Schools Act of 2019—was introduced in the House on January 30 of that year. As of this writing, and according to the tracker on Congress.gov, the legislation remains at the "Introduced" stage. It has yet to pass the House, Senate, go to the president, and become law.

If H.R. 865 were to move from the "Introduced" phase to becoming law, repairing America's schools and stocking them with up-to-date technology and curricular materials would take a massive commitment with big hearts attached. Such an undertaking has been tried before—not in building up schools but in rebuilding a continent.

After World War II, the Marshall Plan dedicated billions of dollars and American dedication and know-how to the effort. George Marshall, who was the secretary of state during this time, said, "Our policy is directed not against any country or doctrine but against hunger, poverty, desperation, and chaos. . . . Political passion and prejudice should have no part."[33]

INTERNATIONAL COMPARISONS

Public-school critics are fond of comparing the United States to other countries that score higher on specific measurements such as the PISA (Programme for International Student Assessment). The PISA data from 79 countries examine 15-year-olds' performances in reading, mathematics, and science. Public-school critics point out that countries such as Finland and Singapore outscore students in the United States on this assessment. The faultfinders do not discuss reasons why Finland and Singapore might shine.

Finland invests in its teachers through stipends, offers early childhood programs to all starting at age 3, and does not subscribe to high-stakes testing. "Imagine what it would be like to teach in a system where you are trusted to assess student progress and help design curriculum!" wrote Neira.[34] It was not uncommon, before *A Nation at Risk* was published, for U.S. teachers to do just what Neira described.

With 10% of the population non-Finnish-speaking,[35] the argument that Finland is more homogeneous than America no longer holds the weight that it once did. Neira visited one school that had a student body composed of 35% immigrants. As for funding, Neira reported, "When it comes to making budget cuts, education isn't touched, regardless of what party's in power."[36]

A former director general of Finland's National Board of Education, Jukka Sarjala, stated:

> What is impressive about Finland's PISA results is not that we provide a high-quality education, but that we provide an education that is both high quality

and high equality. . . . The achievement gap between students from high- and low-income families is . . . relatively small. For us, equality is an economic necessity: the education system must be efficient to develop all talent reserves from all social classes and groups.[37]

Hong grew up in Singapore and attended school in that country from Kindergarten through high school. She describes an unfettered arena where students who don't "measure up" are referred to as "stupid" or "lazy," where pedagogical caning (i.e., the belief that the more a child is whipped, the harder the child will try to achieve) occurs, where parents camp outside for two nights just to get application forms to nursery schools, and where some toddlers are groomed for school interviews by private consultants.[38]

Hong wrote:

In this system, PISA and TIMSS (Trends in Internationals Mathematics and Science Study) scores have become the ultimate goal of education. . . . Ranking is a façade providing merely an illusion of quality and excellence. . . . The focus is far from a cultivation of authentic growth, development, and learning.[39]

The Singaporean system (perhaps minus the name calling and physical punishment) to raise tests scores at all costs seems disturbingly similar to what has transpired in schools—especially underfunded schools—in the U.S. since the accountability movement. Gardner wrote:

No doubt there are things to be learned from effective schools in countries like Finland or Singapore. And yet, the more I have thought about it, the more I have become convinced that the goal of topping the international comparisons is a foolish one, and the rush to raise one's rank a fool's errand. In the process of pursuing a higher rank, educational leaders are ignoring deeper and more important purposes of education.[40]

One must ask the importance of a ranking if nurturing a nation's creativity is not a priority. It is difficult to engage in creative thinking, however, when large chunks of school lessons are devoted to cramming for exams. No one is saying that teaching children how to read and compute—in all senses—is not essential; however, striving to ace a single exam seems counterintuitive to the breadth of knowing.

An online visit to the Smithsonian National Museum of American History exemplifies creative efforts. The Museum houses not only American artifacts that cured the body (e.g., Salk vaccine vials) but also those that continue to delight the being (e.g., Jim Henson's Kermit). A 1942 Harley-Davidson is there, as are Dorothy's ruby slippers. In just the Industry and Manufacturing Collection, the museum houses "thousands of patent models [that] document the creativity of American innovators over more than 200 years."[41] There are some standardized tests among the museum's collections, but there are no examples of students' perfect test results.

NOTES

1. Names of the school, town, pupils, teachers, and administrators are pseudonyms.
2. "CPSB Receives Check for Outstanding Student Test Performance," *Guardian-Journal*, January 23, 2020, 1.
3. "High-Stakes Testing Tips," *Town Talk,* March 11, 2006, www.thetowntalk.com.
4. Michael B. Katz, *Class, Bureaucracy, & Schools: The Illusion of Educational Change in America* (New York: Praeger, 1971), 11.
5. Philip Kotner and Gary Armstrong, *Principles of Marketing,* 7th ed. (Englewood Cliffs, NJ: Prentice Hall, 1996), 595.
6. National Commission on Excellence in Education, *A Nation at Risk: The Imperative for Educational Reform* (Washington, DC: U.S. Government Printing Office, 1983).
7. Anne Bahr Thompson, "Brand Positioning and Brand Creation," in *Brands and Branding*, ed. Rita Clifton and John Simmons (Princeton, NJ: Bloomberg Press, 2003), 79–95.
8. Ibid., 79.
9. Tricia Powell Crain, "76 Alabama Schools on 'Failing' List," updated January 23, 2019, www.al.com.
10. Hoppy Kercheval, "Failing Grades for Many WV Public Schools," *West Virginia Metro News*, September 14, 2018, http://wvmetronews.com/2018/09/14/lousy-grades-for-wv-pubic-schools.
11. Mariana Rodriguez, "Rockford Public Schools Get Failing Grade From the State of Illinois," MyStateLine.com, October 31, 2018, www.mystateline.com/news/rockford-public-schools-get-failing-grade-from-the-state-of-illinois.
12. Brittany Wallman, "Public Schools Get Failing Grades in New Survey by Fort Lauderdale Residents," *South Florida Sun Sentinel*, June 8, 2019, www.sun-sentinel.com/local/broward/fort-lauderdale/fl-ne-fort-lauderdale-schools-20190608poilgxp6nvbyrgxcb72vbevnny-story.html.
13. CBS Austin, "Multiple Austin-Area Schools Earn Failing Grades From Texas Education Agency," August 15, 2019, https://cbsaustin.com/local/multiple-autin-area-schools-earn-failing-grade-from-texas-education-agency.
14. Kristen Taketa, "See If California Has Identified Your School as Low-Performing," *San Diego Union-Tribune*, February 5, 2019, http://sandiegouniontribune.com/news/education/sd-me-worst-performing-schools-20190204-story.html.
15. Dan DeRoos, "Report Cards Are Out for Ohio Schools and 309 Failed," *Cleveland 19*, September 13, 2018, http://cleveland19.com/2018/09/13/report-cards-are-out-ohio-schools-failed.
16. Mike Moffitt, "27 SF Unified Schools 'Low Performing,' Need Improvement, State Says: Nine Are among the Worst in the State," *San Francisco Chronicle,* February 15, 2019, www.sfchronicle.com/education/article/27-SF-Unified-schools-low-performing-education-13611519.php.
17. Mackenzie Ryan, "State: 341 Iowa Schools Are Struggling and Need Comprehensive or Targeted Improvements," *Des Moines Register*, December 18, 2018, www.desmoinesregister.com/story/news/education/2018/12/18/iowa-school-report-card-performance-profiles-every-student-succeeds-act-nclb-needs-improvement/2317321002.
18. Mark Robert Rank, *One Nation, Underprivileged: Why American Poverty Affects Us All* (New York: Oxford University Press, 2006), 37.
19. Brendan Bartanen, Jason A. Grissom, Ela Joshi, and Marc M. Meredith, "Mapping Inequalities in Local Political Representation: Evidence from Ohio School Boards," *AERA Open* 4, no. 4 (December 14, 2018): 1–33, https://journals.sagepub.com/doi/full/10.1177/2332858418818074.

20. Bonnie Johnson, *Wordworks: Exploring Language Play* (Golden, CO: Fulcrum Resources, 1999), 83–86.
21. Jerome H. Skolnick and Elliott Currie, *Crisis in American Institutions,* 11th ed. (Boston: Allyn and Bacon, 2000), 377.
22. Ibid., 376.
23. Tristan Lewis, "Low-Performing Idaho Schools Try to Improve and Turnaround," *Local News 8*, August 22, 2018, https://localnews8.com/news/2018/08/22/low-performing-idaho-schools-try-to-improve-and-turnaround.
24. Liz Riggs, "Why Do Teachers Quit?" *The Atlantic*, October 24, 2013, www.theatlantic.com/education/print/2013/10/why-do-teachers-quit/280699.
25. Josephine Sedgwick, "25-Year-Old Textbooks and Holes in the Ceiling: Inside America's Public Schools," *New York Times*, April 16, 2018, www.nytimes.com/2018/04/16/reader-center/us-public-schools-conditions.html.
26. Debbie Truong, "'Borderline Criminal': Many Public Schools Teeter on the Edge of Decrepitude," *Washington Post*, May 25, 2019, http://washingtonpost.com/local/education/borderline-criminal-thats-the-condition-of-decrepit-public-schools/2019/05/25/bad60064-556f-11e9-814f-e2f46.
27. Liz Bowie, "8 Baltimore City Schools Closed Monday as New Heat, Facility Problems Develop after Weekend Repairs," *Baltimore Sun*, January 8, 2018, www.baltimoresun.com/news/maryland/education/bs-md-ci-city-school-closures-20180108-story.html.
28. Bracey Harris, "Financial Support for Public Schools—and Population—Are Shrinking in Mississippi. Is There an Easy Fix?" *Clarion Ledger*, February 26, 2019, www.mississippitoday.org/2019/02/26/financial-support-for-public-schools-and-population-are-shrinking-in-mississippi-is-there-an-easy-fix.
29. Tajma Hall, "Report Finds Bloomer High School Needs Millions in Repairs," June 25, 2019, www.weau.com/content/news/Report-finds-Bloomer-High-School-in-need-of-millions-in-repairs-511803512.html.
30. PBS News Hour, "Oklahoma Teachers Are Posting Their Crumbling Textbooks Online," April 3, 2018, www.pbs.org/newshour/nation/oklahoma-teachers-are-posting-their-crumbling-textbooks-online.
31. Rachel Cohen, "Public School Buildings Are Falling Apart, and Students Are Suffering for It," *Washington Post*, January 8, 2018, www.washingtonpost.com/news/posteverything/wp/2018/01/08/public-school-buildings-are-falling-apart-and-students-are-suffering/for-it.
32. American Society of Civil Engineers, "Policy Statement 452—Investing in America's Schools," Adopted by the Board of Direction on July 13, 2018, www.asce.org/issues-and-advocacy/public-policy/policy-statement-452-investing-in-america-s-schools.
33. "The Marshall Plan, Speech by US Secretary of State George C. Marshall," June 5, 1947, History and Public Policy Program Digital Archive, Congressional Record, http://digitalarchive.wilsoncenter.org/document/116183.
34. Maria Neira, "We Can Learn from What Finland Is NOT Doing," *New York State United Teachers*, October 2012, 15.
35. Ibid., 15.
36. Ibid., 15.
37. Jukka Sarjala, "Equality and Cooperation: Finland's Path to Success," *American Educator* 37, no. 1 (2013): 32–36.
38. Barbara S. S. Hong, "Seduction of 'East Asian' Schools," in *Alternatives to Privatizing Public Education*, ed. Daniel Ness and Stephen J. Farenga (New York: Routledge, 2017), 189–198.
39. Ibid., 191, 192.
40. Howard Gardner, "Beyond the Herd Mentality: The Minds That We Truly Need in the Future," *Education Week*, September 14, 2005, commentary 44.
41. National Museum of American History, "Industry and Manufacturing," accessed March 2, 2020, https://americanhistory.si.edu/collections/subjects/industry-manufacturing.

Chapter Two

The Realities of an Underfunded School

August, September

TWENTY YEARS AGO

Once a bustling community, the town of Redbud now suffers from a declining population. Cotton and sharecropping drove the economy in the past as did oil; now lumber is the main business. As with many American small towns, the main thoroughfare is lined with abandoned stores.

The editor of the local newspaper reported that of 18,000 in the parish (county), 2,000 are inmates. "The schools don't come any worse than here," she said. "It's poverty—we can't break the cycle. We don't attract industry because the workforce is unskilled, so there are no jobs. Without jobs, how can people improve their lot? They don't even have money to move."

Many Redbud community leaders, African American and White, understand the complexities of poverty—they live among it. The mayor, who grew up in the town, spoke of moral dilemmas that he faces: "If someone doesn't pay the water bill, and the water gets turned off, there will be no water for the children. But if we don't turn the water off, everyone else will want free water. It's a predicament. I don't want to see anybody without water, but I was elected to uphold the laws."

A court official knew of a mother who wanted to give up her newborn child because she could not afford to care for the baby. The official noted, "The barely habitable house had a dirt floor, the water had been turned off, and cardboard covered some of the broken windows. Three hungry-looking siblings played on the floor."

As with the mayor, the court official faced moral dilemmas. She said, "Justice and doing what's right aren't always the same. If people come before a judge arrested for their third DWI, the law says they go to jail. If they go to jail, they can't work, and there's no money for the family. Something has to be done, and I think it's time the churches stood up. The rest of us all have restrictions on what we say. But the churches don't have any restrictions. They are the ones that need to take the lead."

A professional in a nearby correctional institution said, "I wish we would be put out of business. If some of the money shoveled into our end of the pipeline could be rerouted to children for food, decent housing, and well-equipped schools with current textbooks, maybe we could begin to be put out of business."

There are three schools that serve the town and its surroundings. Redbud Elementary is the public school. Deerborne Academy is a private school where the annual tuition rivals that of a small university. Most of Deerborne Academy's students are White. Shady Lake Christian School is another private school that attracts White families. A main benefit of attending Deerborne Academy and Shady Lake Christian School is that their students do not have to take the state standardized test (the LEAP test) and subject themselves to anxiety over the test and possible repetition of a grade for failing this single measure.

REDBUD ELEMENTARY

Redbud Elementary School serves 611 children from preschool through grade 4; 95% of the pupils qualify for free breakfast and free lunch. About 80% of the children are African American. The principal of Redbud Elementary, Pam Porter, is a kindly, effervescent woman who grew up in the area and taught at Redbud for many years. Her gentle manner belies her tenacious stance in what she knows to be best for the children whom she leads.

Many of the children who attend Redbud Elementary are the poorest of the poor. Their homes are substandard and include trailers, shotgun houses, and housing project apartments. Most of the children live with a single parent, an aunt, or a grandmother who hold minimum-wage jobs in fast-food restaurants or a discount store.

There are children at Redbud Elementary who do not receive medical or dental care. Their neighborhood teems with alcohol and drug abuse. Several pupils have witnessed shootings and other types of violence. Despite these conditions, the resilient children of Redbud come to school eager to learn and filled with hope. The children are too young to know the score.

Ms. Porter told two new hires, a third- and a fourth-grade teacher, that the children in the school now wear uniforms. When asked her thoughts on this mode of dress and lack of individual clothing choice, she replied, "There is a child here who wore the same long T-shirt every day to school. It was all she had. The girl told me she was happier now because she looked like the rest of the kids."

During the previous school year, one of the fourth-grade classes at Redbud Elementary had 14 different teachers who stayed from a few days to a few months. Another class had 5 more teachers after the regular teacher resigned midyear. The school is located in a rural town in the Deep South, but it could be in any geographic location where poverty has overtaken all things. Built in 1948, the school's main structure badly needs repairs, paint, and the services of an exterminator.

The school has no library, no counselor, no art classes, no hot water (except for a faucet in the teachers' lounge), inadequate window heating and cooling units, and no regular school nurse. There is no playground equipment except for a few plastic pieces that prekindergarten children use—nothing for the other children.

Redbud Elementary is regulated, monitored, assessed, and labeled by the state's accountability bureaucracy. The school's designation is "academically below average." The spring of 2000 was when *high stakes* took on a serious meaning. Children who failed the state test, given to all public-school children in grades 4 and 8, would have to repeat the grade unless they could pass a retake of the test following a remedial summer session.

Many teachers, especially of grades 4 and 8, reported doing little except preparing their pupils for the test during the months preceding the test dates. Schools and churches in most communities held spirit and pep rallies to encourage students to do well. Some schools and semiprivate or private organizations offered expensive test-prep tutorials for parents and children.

BEFORE THE CHILDREN ARRIVED

The third- and fourth-grade new recruits were experienced teachers. They devoted the first week of August to preparing their rooms for the school year. The third-grade teacher had been assigned to Room B and the fourth-grade teacher to a room down the hall, Room H.

The custodians had just completed their yearly floor waxing (they also mop the floors during the winter break), so the rooms were "ready for occupancy." They were anything but ready. The floors showed over a half century of filth waxed over annually. Apparently, no attempt had been made, at least in recent decades, to remove the buildup of grime from the perimeter and especially the corners of the floors.

The windows, tops of the fluorescent lights, and rickety ceiling fans looked as if they never had been cleaned. Walls looked as if they had not been painted since the construction of the school in 1948. Scuff marks, holes, cracks, tape, falling plaster, and other signs of neglect were everywhere. Parts of the overhead light fixtures were missing.

The ceilings were water stained. In Room B, a large glass section above a wall was broken off, and in another part of the room, a hole offered a view into the adjacent classroom. In the third- and fourth-grade classrooms, the poor fit of the wheezing window air conditioners allowed daylight to come in around the units.

A major job for the new teachers was to rid the rooms of spider webs, some as dense as well-preserved medieval tapestries, in areas of the windows. The rooms were no places for arachnophobes. The teachers sprayed, swatted, and stepped on spiders, some with bodies as large as silver dollars—only thicker and with impressive legs. The spiders were fast, too.

The rooms and hallways had the smell of age with mildew and decades of accumulated dirt prominent. A custodian thought for a moment when he was asked where to get some hot water for scrubbing the walls, the few gouged and scraped bookshelves, and tippy, timeworn student desks. "No place I can think of. There's no hot water in the building. There might be some over there in the high school." The high school was half a block away.

The new teachers, working together, emptied bookshelves to clean them. In the cupboard in Room B, silverfish skittered as they pulled out old student papers, worksheets, and catalogs from some bygone time. A few beetles lumbered out of their well-established homes. Also in Room B sat a sizable unidentifiable piece. The guess was that it served as a bookcase. It resembled a humongous fungus that one might find in a primordial forest. The teachers tried to move the rotting hulk, but it wouldn't budge. They were relieved. Whatever was living under it and behind it would have to wait for another day to be discovered.

The new third- and fourth-grade teachers found basal reading series from 1989 and spelling books from 1986. The language arts, math, science, and social studies materials were of a more recent vintage, having been published in the 1990s. Room B's science equipment consisted of a dusty beaker and a cardboard box of rocks, labeled *Rocks*. Some of the rocks and most of the labels were missing. There were no decorations to make the room cheerful.

In 1952, British prime minister Winston Churchill visited America, Dwight D. Eisenhower was the president-elect, and Ernest Hemingway's *The Old Man and the Sea* was published. It was also the year that the dictionaries the teachers were to use in their classrooms were updated. The copyright date was 1952. In the books, *Alaska* was defined as a U.S. territory, and *Hawaii* wasn't listed (both became states in 1959).

A perusal of the dictionaries uncovered obsolete words such as *hight* and *hitherward*. Some of the entry words were insulting to ethnic groups: *mammy* was defined as "a colored woman in charge of white children; an old Negro woman," and *redskin* was included as the word for "a North American Indian."

The new teachers compared their 1952 dictionaries with a 1997 children's dictionary from home. The latter included *airbag, air conditioner, astronaut, condo, contact lens, fast-food, high-rise, microwave, mouse* (related to computers), *software*, and hundreds of words that have entered the language in the past 50 years. The Redbud dictionaries contained none of these words. In Room H, an even older dictionary, copyright 1941 but not "updated," was found. It had a "new words" section with such entries as *baby sitter, bobby pin, bobby soxer, bulldozer, freezer, juke box, helicopter, iron lung, nylon, penicillin, soap opera,* and *walkie-talkie*.

During the new teachers' cleaning frenzy, several other teachers stopped by to greet them and welcome them to the school. Ruth told them about the many things she bought for her classroom out of her own pocket. "Last year the school provided $200 to each teacher for supplies. But it doesn't go very far. I just paid $8.50 for this poster for my wall. Maybe we'll get $200 again this year, but maybe not. We don't know yet."

Another teacher, Monique, said, "We each get ten reams of paper a year. I run out in the fall, and from then on, I buy my own at a discount store. This year, because of the budget, we may get less paper. There is a list of supplies that each student is to bring from home, such as pencils, markers, notebook paper, and glue. Of course, many students bring nothing. They are too poor. Their unemployed mother may have six or eight other children to worry about. So I go to Wal-Mart and buy the things they need. What else can I do?"

"You have to be careful in Room H," Ruth warned. "Last year I bought some shrimp eggs for the kids to watch for science class. One morning most of the eggs were missing. I discovered a long line of ants carrying them outside through the hole in the wall. Did you see the hole?" The new teachers had seen the hole.

Belinda, a third-grade teacher, added, "There have been rats going between Rooms B and C in the past."

"I don't deal well with rodents," said Nikki with a wry grin. She was the teacher assigned to Room C. The new recruits commented that they weren't exactly the Pied Pipers of Hamelin either.

Ruth reported that last year there was a sample state test question on the use of a thesaurus. There are no thesauri for the children. The teachers had to create worksheet lessons on the thesaurus to accommodate the presumed upcoming questions on the test.

The new teachers asked Ruth about classes such as art, music, and physical education; she said that there were no art classes, but there is a "gifted art program." Children take a test to see if they are artistically inclined. Those children go to the high school occasionally for art. When asked what percentage of the children pass the test, she reported, "There was just one child last year in my class who passed. He was really talented. There were 15 in the whole school." Ruth also mentioned that the music teacher probably would not be coming back and that they still needed to hire a physical education teacher.

Jane, a first-grade teacher just out of college, was a part of the conversation. She looked at everyone, at the condition of the room, at the outdated materials, had heard the news about the special art classes, the ant brigade and the darting rats, and said in a tiny voice, "I'm scared."

The children come from almost indescribable poverty. Ruth said that in her 2 years on the faculty, only two students, one per year, had to pay a reduced lunch fee. All other children had qualified for free breakfast and free lunch. She added, "I live near the apartments where a number of our students live. It's rough. Many times I'll see third and fourth graders out on the streets at 10:30 or 11:00 at night. They are unsupervised. They come to school hungry and dirty. Some fall asleep in class."

Ruth explained that the tired air conditioners in the rooms are also the heating units, which are needed especially in December, January, and February. "Last year the units often broke down, leaving the room without heat for several weeks. One little girl had no coat, so I gave her one that my cousin had outgrown. She wore it every day for over a month and then started wearing it inside out. She refused to take it off until it got very warm. One day when she was at recess, I peeked inside the coat. There was some paint on it. Apparently the child didn't want to hurt my feelings, so she wore the coat inside out."

Ruth continued, "Many of the children who have coats don't want to take them off in school. Maybe it's because the coats are security blankets for them or maybe it's because they have something they can call their own and don't want to lose them."

Martha, a veteran second-grade teacher, told the new teachers that she kept blankets in her room. "Some children come to school with high fevers and chills. No one will pick them up or there is no one at home. I try to keep them warm with blankets. I just ache for them. They have to sit at their desks, heads down and very sick, because there is no place for them to lie down." The school has no nurse's room or cots.

That afternoon, the new third- and fourth-grade teachers began to wade through the Redbud Elementary teacher handbook. The handbook has more than 100 pages packed with information, including emergency telephone numbers, faculty addresses, philosophies of the school district, the school calendar, and an assortment of rules and regulations. Among the school rules are the following:

- "Breakfast duty begins at 7:15 and ends at 7:55. There should be an empty row of tables dividing the high school students and elementary students."
- "Restroom breaks for fourth grade will be from 10:05-10:15, 1:00-1:15, and 2:40-2:50 P.M." [Actually, there are only two restroom breaks.]
- "Boys and girls are assigned to different areas on the playground. Teacher in charge is to have students follow playground rules and keep students in designated area." [Recall that there is no playground equipment at Redbud Elementary.]
- "At lunch teachers, unless otherwise assigned, will go to the cafeteria with their class daily. Noise should be kept to a minimum in the cafeteria." [Teachers are responsible for cleaning their class's table(s) after the children have finished eating.]
- "Throwing rocks, dirt, pinecones, or sticks on the playground is not permitted due to the possibility of student injury."

There are many more pages of rules that regulate the daily lives of the teachers. Lesson planning, for example, requires, among many other things, correlating the plans to the appropriate content standards and benchmarks. There are rules that specify the precise number of minutes per week that are to be devoted to each subject area. For example, in grade 3, language arts is to be taught for 165 minutes, 5 days a week.

Although not in the handbook, teachers new to the school were warned by other teachers that the neighborhood was especially dangerous after 5:00 p.m. because of the crack cocaine trade, drive-by shootings, and robberies.

AUGUST/SEPTEMBER: THE CHILDREN OF ROOMS B AND H

Week 1, August 21–25: The Daily Routine

Third and Fourth Grades

The children arrived today. Twenty-one bright-eyed girls and boys in school uniforms found their desks in Room B, third grade. Twenty-two others made their way to fourth grade, Room H. The school uniforms are varied. Choices include red, white, blue, or plaid tops and navy or khaki bottoms. The pupils wear pants, shorts, or skirts. Some children carry their required school supplies (scissors, glue, notebook paper, pencils, crayons, and so on), but several children are empty-handed.

Third and fourth graders come in all shapes and sizes. The teachers learn quickly that their levels of reading and writing are as dissimilar as their heights and weights. Rosters show that 6 of the 21 third graders are in special education, as are four of the fourth graders. These children are nonreaders. Of the 21 third graders, only four are approaching reading on a third-grade level. In the fourth grade, about half the children are reading at the fourth-grade level, according to a quick pretest.

Among the 22 fourth graders is Dwayne, a slender boy with a ready smile and a timid demeanor. Joshua, one of five White children in the class, is quick with his hand in the air and filled with questions and suggestions. De'Lewis appears nervous as he stacks and restacks his crayons on his desk. His mother accompanies him on that first morning and urges, "Stay on top of him. But you can't reach me. I'm (at work) all day. Last year the school tried to call me too much."

Among the third graders, there are five White children. The African American pupils and the White children mix freely. Third graders, at least in this classroom, seem to be unconcerned about skin color. A few personalities stand out from the others. Manuel and Jaron talk loudly and nonstop. Jelani is swatting his neighbor. Keaziah is running around the room. Leon is playing with a metal pull cord from a lamp. The rest of the children are seated and staring toward the front of the room in anticipation.

Teachers work the entire day with practically no break from their classes. When it is their weekly duty day, they are with the children from 7:15 a.m. until 3:35 p.m. when the last bus leaves. On other days, start-up time is 7:55 a.m. The teachers accompany the children to and from their 10-minute recess and to the two bathroom breaks (following recess and lunch), and they walk with their children half-a-block to the cafeteria building and eat with them there.

Just 30 minutes are allotted to march to the cafeteria, wash all hands in a trough, stay in line to get food, gobble down the meal, return the trays, and walk as a group to the bathrooms. Classes that have music or physical education after lunch have only 20 minutes for the entire procedure.

Each teacher's only break from class comes during the 25 minutes daily when the class has music or physical education. The teacher must, however, walk the children to the music room, which is in a portable classroom at the far end of the main building, and then return to the portable building to walk them back. On alternate days, students are walked to the gym. Net "free time" per day is 10 minutes. This is when the teacher must use the restroom (one for the faculty and staff of 72), as there is no other time during the day. It is also during this "planning time" when teachers are expected to return or make phone calls to parents.

The area is in the thick of a scorching heat wave. Records are broken daily as temperatures soar above 100 degrees. The intense sun beats down on the dry, cracked playground as the 200 third and fourth graders run out for their 10-minute recess. Most pupils run around under the relentless sun, playing tag or throwing the one or two rubber balls that a child brings from home.

Teacher voices can be heard above the din, reminding fourth-grade boys not to go near the softball diamond because "that's not ours." As a security measure, girls are warned to stay away from the far fences. Children who fall on the hard ground have scrapes and cuts. Here and there a child cries because of an injury or, more often, because of an insult from another child. The insults usually refer to a child's mother (e.g., "Your mama is a crackhead") or a deceased relative. All too quickly they must line up again by class for the march to the bathrooms or, for third graders, to their classrooms.

Even though it is just the first week of school, the teachers know that if they could work one-on-one with some of the children, the pupils could learn to read and write. Chalese is a fourth grader who is a nonreader and nonwriter. She knows two sight words—*go* and *look*—and can write a few letters, some of them backward. Chalese, like many of the children, yearns for attention. She often comes to the teacher's desk to proudly show her scribbles. If Chalese received the attention that she craves, she could succeed.

A few children, however, seem to have given up as early as the third grade. Most of the nonreaders simply do not attempt to do anything. They sit and snip paper, play with glue, and doodle. Any type of written material is ignored. Fourth graders De'Lewis, Antron, and Tony do nothing until prodded and hounded by the teacher; however, each of the three has shown that he can read and write a little.

Third graders Leon, Kanzah, and Chikae cannot read even one word. Their writing consists of random letters that make no sense. By age 8, they have stopped trying. They spend their class time drawing and pestering others or just staring into space.

While lining up to enter the building one morning, third grader Cherise asks if she will get a warning if she falls asleep in class. She is told that she will not. "Our neighbor in the next apartment played music until one o'clock last night," she reports.

Wendice and Leon fall asleep in their third-grade classroom every day this week. Wendice is lethargic and has a deep cough. He complains of chest pains. Leon, who constantly is in motion, wears himself out by noon. Fourth grader Yolanda has to be awakened every day. Most of the pupils report bedtimes of 11 o'clock, midnight, or later.

There are three computers in each classroom. In the third-grade room, two are broken, and the one with an Internet connection has lost the connection. The overhead projector has a three-prong plug, but the electrical outlet accommodates only two prongs.

A group of fourth graders reads a story about a boy whose mother dies and whose father later remarries. The child in the story isn't sure about this stepmother, but eventually the two agree they can be friends. When asked if any of them have stepmothers or stepfathers, two pupils reply that they have stepmothers. Dwayne grimaces. "I hate her. She don't like me."

Derek joins in. "Mine was so bad my dad dumped her. She had tattoos all over and metal in the skin. She was awful." Demetrius later confides to his fourth-grade teacher, "I live with my mama and daddy, but mostly I live with my aunt. My mama had five babies and they was too much for her. I like living at my aunt's house."

The first week closes with 109-degree temperatures and two broken water fountains. Redbud children return from recess, lunch, and the non-air-conditioned gym with no water to drink. Driving back home after school, the two new teachers hear the radio broadcaster warning listeners to make sure their pets have plenty of drinking water.

It irks the teachers when they think of their morning drive past a magnificent church that sits on lush, green acreage. In the middle of a record-setting heat wave and drought, the church's underground water sprinklers work overtime lavishing precious water on its golf-course-like grass carpets. On the weekend, teachers stock up on paper cups so their pupils can at least drink some tepid water from a faucet in the building.

A large part of the upcoming weekend will be spent poring over a pile of forms and memoranda. These are handed out during an after-school meeting. Teachers wish that they could spend more time preparing useful instructional activities for their pupils—especially for the nonreaders who have given up. Instead, their time will be spent looking up codes for standards, benchmarks, activities, modifications, and assessments and attaching these codes to instructional plans.

Teachers had been warned by Mr. Green, a district administrator, that he could come at any time to check their plan books for these codes. There will be little time left for actual meaningful planning. In just 1 week, the new teachers have come to understand that a major culprit hampering the education of children and souring the professional lives of teachers is useless state-mandated busywork.

Week 2, August 28–September 1: The Heat Wave Continues

Third Grade

Jimmy is coughing and complaining of chest pains. The teacher asks him if he has told his mother. He says that he has. "Have you seen a doctor?" she inquires. "No," he mumbles. Many children complain of tooth pain. Cherise has tears running from her eyes. She isn't crying; she is in pain. The teacher asks how many children have been to a dentist. Only 5 of the 21 raise their hands. Every day some of the pupils report stomachaches. This is attributed to hunger.

Each day the teacher reads to the class, usually just before lunch. Four or five children fall into a deep sleep during this time. Some sleep so soundly that it is difficult to wake them for lunch.

In previous years, Pam Porter has been in charge of her over 600-pupil school with no administrative assistance. Now there is a new face. Greta Dawson has been hired as an assistant principal in charge of discipline. At an after-school meeting, Ms. Dawson introduces the faculty to her three-strikes method of discipline. Strike 1 is a warning, strike 2 requires that the child be isolated from the rest of the class for the day, and strike 3 means being sent to Ms. Dawson's office for a lecture, a paddling, or suspension. Within days, pupils learn that they do not want to be sent to Ms. Dawson.

Ms. Dawson is a statuesque woman capable of a warm, inviting smile and a hug for a kindergartener or a scary scowl. Three signs rotate on her office door: a smiley face, a frowning face, and a weeping face. No one is sure if they indicate her mood that day or if they suggest what's happening behind her closed door.

Ms. Dawson is not shy about telling teachers how to discipline their classes. On the playground, she tells them firmly and up close, "Don't let children lie on the ground!" One always can tell when Ms. Dawson is in the vicinity; small heads turn in unison, and little eyes grow big. Usually accompanying Ms. Dawson is a string of students, some silent and chagrined, others weeping. Misbehavior in the cafeteria means standing at attention on a square tile in front of all the students. The effect is similar to the stocks or dunking stool in days of yore. Third grader Jelani says, "She mean. She everywhere."

There are three after-school curriculum-related meetings this week. Tuesday's meeting is an attempt by local teachers to wade through the math standards and benchmarks and to key and sequence objectives to 6-week periods for each grade level. All teachers, however, must find and note the resources they use to meet these objectives. The math objectives do not sequentially correlate to any math books available in the school. There is no money for additional resources other than the rumored $200 per year per teacher. The meeting ends at 5:15 p.m.

On Wednesday after school, teachers are shown how to do "running records," a method for evaluating the oral reading of an individual child using an elaborate system of coding. This technique was intended to be an informal, quick measure for the teacher's use. Now mandated, it has become cumbersome.

The district wants each teacher to test each child individually using a running record analysis several times during the year. One teacher whispers, "When will we find the time to teach? All we do is test." Most of the teachers already know the children's reading levels through several days of observation and oral and written work. The meeting drags on until 5:30 p.m.

The DRA (Developmental Reading Assessment) is the topic of Thursday's after-school session. This assessment requirement is state mandated. It is to be given individually twice a year to every child in the classroom. In theory, the DRA would give a teacher about the same information as the running record procedure; however, the coding system is entirely different, time consuming, and elaborate. Any elementary school teacher could diagnose children's reading difficulties through informal observation; undergraduate students are taught how to do just that. None of these complicated evaluation systems are necessary.

The meeting ends at 5:40 p.m. In the state, elementary students must take the Iowa Test of Basic Skills annually, the high-stakes state test in fourth and eighth grades, the individually administered DRA assessment twice annually, and the individually administered running records assessments several times annually. Teachers wondered which high-powered sales reps or product promoters had such success convincing people in the state capitol to burden teachers and frustrate and frighten children with so much unnecessary formal testing.

It is announced that in addition to the balanced literacy training that teachers had before school started, and the previously mentioned after-school training this week, week 4 would include 3 days of after-school training in a particular phonics methodology. On the drive home, the new teachers agreed that if they were not experienced educators, they would reconsider their career choice. No wonder the scores in the state are so low. There is no time to teach. All worry about how many of the teachers will stick it out until the end of the school year.

Fourth Grade

Victavius arrives at 7:15 a.m. with tears running down his cheeks. He is asked what's wrong. "My ear hurts." The teacher knows that the district school nurse comes once a week and has already been there this week. Victavius calls his mother. "She'll come at 10:30," he reports. His face is contorted in pain. By noon, no mother.

Ruth had Victavius in class last year. She knows a cousin of the boy and contacts her. "I can't find his mother, and his grandmother is drunk," says the cousin. At 2:30, the cousin finds the mother—inebriated. The mother rides to school with a friend to pick up Victavius. Ruth explains to the new hire that Victavius's older brother was shot and killed earlier in the summer and that the mother has been drinking since that time. She has four other children.

The second week of school begins with a temperature of 107 degrees and ends with a record-setting 111 degrees. The state has had no rain in August and half an inch in July. The grass is brown, and the deciduous trees are losing their leaves. Burn bans are in effect. One benefit of all the heat is that there are fewer huge cockroaches to squash before the children arrive.

The class is discussing the Pecos Bill tall tale and shows an interest in rodeos. The teacher mentions that the major state men's penitentiary, Angola, holds a rodeo each year with the inmates as participants. Tony raises and waves his hand. "I know about Angola. My daddy there." The child says that he'll ask his father about the rodeo during the next phone call to him in prison.

Week 3, September 5–8: More Codes

Third and Fourth Grades

Pupils are never far from teachers' minds. On Saturday the two new hires go to a mega-bookstore to look for a rhyming dictionary and an idiom dictionary. They notice that the children's section is filled with healthy, vibrant, mostly White children, many of whom are being read to by adults. Several of the children choose books for purchase. The teachers think of their students, most of whom own no books and probably have never seen the inside of a bookstore.

The heat wave broils on. The gym is 120 degrees—a teacher brings a thermometer. The loud classroom air conditioners pant out some cool air. The new teachers learn from a friend in a Chicago suburb that her children's school closed at noon in the 90-degree heat because the children were "getting light headed." There is no talk of light-headedness among the children of poverty taking physical education in a 120-degree gym. The drivers report that it is also 120 degrees or higher on their non-air-conditioned buses.

On Tuesday there is another after-school meeting. This one is held to describe a new coding system for the state English/language arts standards and benchmarks. Each elementary teacher in the district is given a packet the size of a ream of paper.

The document lists 326 different English-language objectives, each one keyed to the state test, the Iowa Test of Basic Skills, the Bloom taxonomy, and a "Strand." Also listed are the hours it should take to teach the objectives and a blank space for the teachers to write the resources they use to achieve the objective.

Here is an example:

This objective is categorized as being at the analysis level on Bloom's taxonomy and is allotted 2.0 hours for instruction.

Not only is this list dizzying to the teachers expected to teach it (especially with most of the children well below grade level), but it is also riddled with ambiguities. It cannot be discerned how the "syllabication" objective is

| 5. Syllabication | Inference | Fourth Content Standard |
| distinguish syllables in words | | (ELA-1-E1/pg 2 #4)/LEAP/IOWA |

related to the Strand "inference" or to the "analysis" level on Bloom's taxonomy because syllabication is simply a pronouncing task.

The packet also contains a 42-page curriculum grade book spreadsheet that lists each of the 326 objectives followed by "days 1–30." It is to be used by the teachers to track what they teach and when they teach it. This is how the state interprets the concept of "teacher accountability." All the previously mentioned material is to be fed by teachers into their weekly lesson plan books, and it is to direct their classroom instruction. There are no materials available, however, that are keyed—sequentially or topically—to the objectives document.

The presenter urges teachers to list the resources that they use when they teach each objective. "At the end of the year, these resources will be shared with a compiling committee so that other teachers may get your great ideas," she woos. The previous week teachers received one of these behemoths for math, too, and more are promised for social studies and science.

The person who presents the English-language standards is a middle-school teacher from another district. She admonishes, "You must teach to mastery all the objectives that will be tested on the LEAP (state test) and Iowa test. Skip the others until after the tests next March. We have no time to teach fluff." It has become clear even to the most optimistic that school is no longer for education. Schools are now test prep centers, and woe be to those who don't do enough prepping.

As the new teachers leave their meeting after 5:00 p.m., they notice, as they have on many late days, how the neighborhood atmosphere changes and takes on the feel of "mean streets." Clusters of thin men congregate outside seemingly vacant houses—crack houses, they are told. The teachers are reminded of what veteran Redbud teachers said at the beginning of the school year: "Don't drive around the neighborhood after 5:00. It just becomes too dangerous."

Third Grade

While on the 7:15 a.m. playground duty, the new recruit speaks with Belinda, who has taught for more than 30 years. Belinda says that she feels helpless when teaching higher-order thinking skills. "They have so little background knowledge. They have so little to build on. It is sad." The farthest most of the students have been from Redbud is a town about 20 miles away. "You have to go to the Wal-Mart in Minden. They got everything." Their eyes light up as they say this. Many want to work at Wal-Mart when they grow up.

A form to be completed by parents or guardians requests information such as current work and home telephone numbers. The sheets continue to trickle back to school. Many parents are working poor. They work at fast-food restaurants, at a discount store, or as chicken deboners at a local plant. One sheet reads, "unploy."

Third and Fourth Grades

The pupils need help in developing listening skills. Speaking and listening development are not tested on the paper-and-pencil state test, and thus the state probably will ignore them. This is a critical mistake because speaking and listening are two crucial building blocks of learning. Listening comprehension parallels and precedes reading comprehension. Speaking parallels and precedes writing development. These integral components of language now are presumably considered "fluff" and will be skipped in many classrooms by well-intentioned but pressured teachers.

Both classes complete a student survey in which they are asked to respond to a number of questions. One item asks them to describe "the number one problem today." Replies include "drugs," "drinking," "guns," "knives," "killing," and "the LEAP test." Others write "violence in school" and "school shootings." Another question asks what they would make disappear if they could. Answers include "sticks and rats," "barking dogs," "old shoes," "my brother's disease," and "the water bill."

Third Grade

Jaron reports that he saw a second-grade boy stick out his tongue at an adult when her back was turned. The teacher asks the class what they think about someone doing this. Jaheesa says, "If you do that to somebody when you grow up, you could get shot." Violence is never too far away from the minds of the 8-year-olds.

After school, the new-to-the-district teacher helps another third-grade teacher, Glenda, with her lesson plans. Even after 14 years of teaching the age group, Glenda is told, the plans take the experienced teacher an entire Saturday to complete because of the accountability requirements.

Something is terribly wrong with Wendice. His coughing has subsided somewhat, but he complains of a painful jaw. He continues to sleep in class. There is a pus-filled sore on his left arm. The teacher asks him about it. He tells her that he has a lot of these sores on his feet. She takes him into the hall and has him remove his shoes and socks. Several sores cover his tiny feet. The teacher sends for Ms. Dawson. The child must have medical attention. Ms. Dawson takes Wendice away.

Week 4, September 11–16: Getting Students' Attention

Fourth Grade

While on late bus duty, the teacher tells a kindergartener to sit down. This is done for safety reasons. With bus and carpool traffic coming and going in front of the building, there is the constant fear of a child darting out in front of a vehicle. The kindergartener tells the teacher, "I can't sit down. I got new pants on." The legs of the pants have been rolled up several times to allow for growth. The child is shown how to squat so he won't get his pants dirty or torn. The little guy squats for 15 minutes until his bus arrives.

Third Grade

Wendice is absent today, and Kanzah is crying from tooth pain. The teacher requests that the school nurse come to school and look at his tooth. It is broken and black.

New (to the district) teachers have three after-school meetings this week from 3:30 to 5:00 p.m. They are to learn about Project Read, the phonics program used at Redbud Elementary. Then from 5:00 to 6:30 p.m., there is a meeting of the Parent-Teacher Organization (PTO).

Third and Fourth Grades

The PTO begins with Pam Porter introducing the faculty and staff. She states, "I sent a letter to every parent in the district asking for volunteers to serve as PTO officers this year. Not one person responded." It is easy to see that there are more teachers and staff in attendance than parents. Teachers count about 30 unfamiliar faces, whom they presume are parents. There are over 600 pupils in the school. Ms. Porter continues, "I hope you will think about serving and let me know before our next meeting."

The new reading program is described, and several teachers tell about class reading projects. Only one parent asks a question, and it pertains to the state test. Teachers and parents alike seem thankful when the meeting ends at 6:00 and they can leave the sweltering gym.

On the drive home, the two new hires discuss the previous evening's *60 Minutes* segment on the high-stakes TAAS test required in the state of Texas. The program emphasized the frenzy surrounding the test. It showed pep rallies, marching bands, special hats worn by children, and flags all designed to rev kids up—not for a football game but for the TAAS test. Texas teachers were interviewed. They expressed their outrage over what has happened to schooling in Texas because of the tests. One teacher reported that her school has no library but spent $20,000 on test-preparation materials.

The program highlighted the pressures placed on children. A small child who was interviewed was crying because the next day he had to take the test. CBS reporter Leslie Stahl commented that school administrators can receive a $25,000 annual bonus for improving TAAS scores.

Educators lamented that real teaching and learning can no longer occur in Texas. All efforts must be directed toward passing the multiple-choice TAAS test. The new teachers believe that this practice will come back to haunt the businesspeople promoting it when there are no divergent, creative thinkers to move their enterprises forward. Will the schools and teachers then be blamed for these serious shortfalls?

Third Grade

The teacher learns from the school nurse that Wendice has impetigo. His mother says that she cannot afford to take him to a doctor. He stays out of school the rest of the week.

Fourth Grade

The students change classes once a day. The new recruit teaches reading/language arts and social studies to his homeroom from 8:00 until 10:40 a.m. Then he and Kay Henderson change classes; she teaches math and science to his class while he teaches reading/language arts and social studies to her class. Kay is a retired educator with a doctoral degree who used to teach at the local prison. She was coaxed into coming out of retirement because of the elementary teacher shortage in the state.

Each day the two teachers compare notes and wonder what they could be doing to better capture their students' attention and interests. Are they expecting too much? Their hearts understand the difficult living conditions that the children come from, but their heads tell them that if the pupils only would listen and follow directions, they could be helped and maybe escape the entrenched poverty in Redbud. A staff member tells the two teachers at recess that the children come from environments with constant noise. "All they are used to is people shouting at them," she says.

Week 5, September 18–22: Wasting Instructional Time

Third and Fourth Grades

On Saturday, the new teachers invest in a reading rug for each classroom: Wal-Mart, five by eight, $28.88 per rug. The children are ecstatic. Initially, they won't walk on the rugs but take circuitous routes around them. During their reading times on the rugs, some children pick grass and other debris from the rugs and fluff them up with their hands.

Third Grade

This morning before school starts, a tearful grandmother is waiting by Room B. She tells the teacher that Gerard's mother has taken him away and that she is here to gather up his things. Gerard is a nervous little boy who often mentioned his younger sister. She died "because something was wrong with her heart," he said.

Kanzah is crying again with a terrible toothache. On Tuesday morning, the school nurse checks his rotting, black molar. She tries to call his home, but the phone has been disconnected. She gives Kanzah a letter to take home. It states that the child needs immediate care. The following day Kanzah hands his teacher a note that says, "This is Kanzah grandmother. I am going to make him apnement for his teeth today. Thank you."

Fourth Grade

The teacher receives a letter from a parent that tells about practices "to which I take religious exception to. . . . The practices we feel are contrary to our religious beliefs include any stories and activities that include fairies, trolls, and such to include all Harry Potter materials."

Third Grade

The new hire still is working on the Development Reading Assessments. Sometimes a child can take an entire day to find a small DRA booklet with which he or she feels comfortable. Teachers are trained to know where to place children in reading materials. There is so much testing going on that the amount of time for teaching is shamefully reduced.

The teacher feels guilty taking precious instructional time away from the pupils to fulfill these testing requirements. She knows better. The exasperating truth is that the individually administered DRA given in grades 1, 2, and 3; the high-stakes state test given in grades 4 and 8; and the Iowa test given in nearly all grades are required by the state for accountability purposes—not as evaluative tools to help teachers.

The third-grade teachers have an after-school meeting at which record-keeping is discussed. At the end of the meeting, Ms. LeGrande is writing in a notebook. The new hire asks her what she is doing. She says, "I have to document that we are having this meeting." The message is clear: Someone doesn't trust teachers to do their jobs. They must document everything. Teachers continue to be disturbed by the oppressive amounts of monitoring that occur at every level of education. The implicit message is that people in authority mistrust educators and must be shown "proof" of their compliance with every rule and regulation.

In a group of four, the children and their teacher are reading a short book about the human body. They discuss bones and muscles. Shantel asks about black eyes. "They're bruises," the teacher tells her.

"My mama got a black eye because some man hit her. Then some other man came and held on to the guy who hit her. She hit him hard on the head. Then somebody called the police."

Week 6, September 25–29: Grades and Motivation

Third and Fourth Grades

On the drive to Redbud Elementary, the two new-to-the-district teachers lament the low grades of many of their students. It is the 6th week of school, and report cards are sent home every 6 weeks. Letter grades must be given as well as percentage scores based on classwork and homework. The teachers spent part of the weekend adding up each student's points in each subject and calculating the percentage scores.

To their disappointment, close to half of their students were destined to receive Ds or Fs on their first report card of the year. They worry that the low grades will squelch motivation; however, they are compelled by state and district mandates to teach to the standards and benchmarks and adhere to the grading policies.

Third Grade

In social studies the discussion is about ancestors. "My grandma's ancestor was a slave in Shreveport," report Jaron. Several of the children chime in to say that they, too, have slaves as ancestors.

"When did slaves get free?" asks Manuel.

"During the Civil War, a war between the northern and southern states," the teacher replies.

"Were you around then?" inquires Manuel.

"No, I'm not that old," she responds.

"Were you sort of around then?" he continues. The teacher tells him that she would have to be at least 140 years old to have witnessed the Civil War. Antinesha asks if Dr. Martin Luther King Jr. helped free the slaves. The teacher briefly explains the Civil Rights Movement and tells them that the movement came long after the Civil War and that she does remember Dr. King.

Fourth Grade

Twenty parents show up for the 5:00 p.m. meeting to discuss the upcoming state test. They represent about one out of six of the fourth graders. Handouts prepared by the fourth-grade teachers are passed around, as is a list of websites with relevant instructional materials. Even though most of the parents do not have computers at home, the Redbud Public Library has several. The parents of the children who are the farthest behind academically are not in attendance.

Third Grade

Tuesday after school, the third-grade teachers meet with Pam Porter and Kim Bridges, the reading specialist. Ms. Porter reminds them that members of the central office will begin visiting classrooms, unannounced, in October to review their coded lesson plans. Central office personnel will make certain that teachers are teaching Project Read, the phonics program to which new (to the district) teachers have just been introduced.

Third and Fourth Grades

Today it was announced that all third- and fourth-grade teachers will be required to attend a 4-hour session next week Thursday after school from 3:30 to 7:30 p.m. Its purpose will be to train teachers in a new, complex computer program designed to help them "pinpoint" their students' needs and to offer computerized instruction addressing those needs. The teachers wonder where the add-on will fit into their fragmented schedules. They learn that the district will spend $85,500 for this software.

Teachers have been with their children for 6 weeks, and they know what they need. What they need most is more personal interaction. The quality of this latest gimmick remains to be seen. Teachers continue to be surprised by the number of computer and publishing ventures, consultants, "implementation teams," and similar groups that have come to feed at the standards-and-accountability trough. They think of the 1952 dictionaries and the absence of thesauri in their classrooms. And the school has no library.

Fourth Grade

The children like to take their shoes off when they read on the reading rug. Dario comes up to the teacher and whispers, "Verlin say bad things about my socks." Dario's socks are filthy and holey. The teacher tells him not to let the comment bother him and says, "There will be no talking about socks if you want to be on the reading rug."

Chapter Three

Regulating Teaching

October

Week 7, October 2–6: No Money for School Pictures

Third Grade

This morning before the children arrive, the teacher is swinging a broom at one of the jumbo cockroaches that greet her every day. "Just look at what you're doing," she says to herself. Her morning extermination routine has become commonplace. Tonight is the evening of the 4-hour after-school workshop on how to use the software package that is intended to help children pass the state test.

The teacher thinks of the moldy, insect-infested room that she is working in and the lack of hot water for hand-washing. She thinks of having to beg and borrow any type of appropriate print material for the children. She thinks of no playground equipment or art classes. What computer program could be so powerful that it should come before the children's basic needs?

Third and Fourth Grades

School pictures are taken. Students who wish to purchase pictures bring their money in a special envelope provided by the photography studio. Only 1 of the 22 students in the fourth-grade homeroom brings picture money and only 1 child of the 20 students in the third-grade classroom. The remainder will have no photographic record of this year at Redbud Elementary. The pupils sit and smile for the photographer as he takes the pictures that never will belong to them.

A consultant for the new balanced literacy reading program spends a day at Redbud Elementary giving demonstration lessons for each grade level. She is reminiscent of the consultants who preceded her this year. The consultant sits with three to five of the best readers and asks them questions about a storybook. Meanwhile, the rest of the class exhibits sterling behavior as they work in centers. No doubt the presence of the principal and five or six teachers who are there to see the consultant "orchestrate balanced literacy" contribute to their model deportment.

The building-wide consensus among teachers was that the day was a flop. The consultant had demonstrated an aspect of the program that we all knew how to do. There isn't a teacher in the land who can't work with a small group of good readers. All the hard stuff was avoided by the consultant. Questions such as what to do with nonreaders in centers were dismissed with "even kindergarteners can do centers."

Third Grade

The teacher reads a book about Thurgood Marshall to the children. They discuss segregation and discrimination. Antinesha tells the class that her aunt and uncle were thrown in jail during the Civil Rights Movement. "For what?" she is asked.

"For doing this," she replies. She stands up and carries an imaginary picket sign. "Oh, they were marching for civil rights," the teacher says. Antinesha nods.

"I'm afraid of the Ku Klux Klan," reports Leon. "They burned down a house of an old lady. They kill people." The other children agree.

In the book about Thurgood Marshall, the children notice a sign that says "Colored" with an arrow pointing to the left. They ask the teacher what that means. She says, "'Colored' is what people used to call Blacks or African Americans."

"Why 'Colored'?" asks Chikae.

Manuel points to his face and replies, "Because we got color."

"Oh yeah," said Chikae.

The children are on the rug as the teacher reads the book to them. They begin to compare the colors of the skin on their arms.

"Each color is different," said Manuel.

The children seem intrigued and pleased with these differences.

There was an armed robbery at the local Piggly Wiggly grocery store. The suspect wore a camouflage ski mask and carried a semiautomatic handgun. He forced employees into the cooler and removed money from the safe. The children are all atwitter about this robbery because so many of them go to the Piggly Wiggly. Jaron says, "I saw a robbery before. The police shot two guys in the legs when they tried to run away."

Third and Fourth Grades

At the start of the 4-hour after-school workshop on the newly purchased computer program, teachers ask how much it cost. The technology person for the district responds, "Well, it was expensive."

"How expensive?" they prod.

"Well we got a matching grant, and then we finagled some, so we got it for $85,500, but it should have cost us almost half a million dollars." Teachers ask her who the authors of the program are and what their credentials are.

She says, "I don't know. It was correlated to a lot of tests."

"Is this another test-prep program?" teachers ask. They explain how fragmented the curriculum is. "We can already pinpoint the needs of our students; this is the seventh week of school," the teachers state.

"Maybe you can, but most teachers can't."

"Yes, they can," is the response.

The technology person responds in whispered tones, "Well, the word is, you should really only teach reading and math because of the ... test."

"Isn't anyone worried about effects of depriving children of science, social studies, and the arts?" teachers inquire.

"Well, just integrate everything through the reading," the technologist advises.

As the teachers sit through the presentation by the consultant who sold this program, they quickly become aware that the software is little more than high-tech skill-and-drill. Each aspect of reading, math, and other disciplines has been fractioned into its tiniest subcomponents on which the students take practice tests, complete drill lessons, and then take posttests. Occasionally there is a paragraph to read and a short essay to write.

There are elaborate mechanisms for assigning students to various levels of pretests on numerous subskills to "pinpoint their needs" and then other mechanisms to assign them to various categories of instruction. When the consultant is asked if there is something in the program for our nonreaders at all grade levels, she replies, "No, this program doesn't teach them to read. Your district didn't buy that program. If you're interested, we have another program—a computerized phonics program—for sale that will teach them to read."

At exactly 7:30 p.m., the consultant ends her presentation by apologizing for having talked too fast. "This actually should be a nine-hour workshop that I have crammed into four hours. On page 3 of the handout is my e-mail address. I don't give out my phone number. If you have problems, call Peggy [the district technologist]. Sometimes the best thing you can do is to just turn the computer off and start over again."

Week 8, October 9–13: Parent Conferences and Professional Growth Plans

Fourth Grade

Today the fourth-grade classes each received a classroom set of dictionaries and thesauri. The teachers had been asking for these reference books since before the school year began. The superintendent was able to use some money from a tobacco settlement in the state. Only the fourth grade is given the new books, and that is because of the state test. Third graders must be content with their 1952 dictionaries and no thesauri.

Third and Fourth Grades

An advertisement was spotted in the October 5 issue of the local Redbud newspaper announcing "job vacancies" for a third-grade teacher and a fourth-grade teacher. No teacher at Redbud Elementary has resigned yet, but two of the teachers at Redbud announced that they will not be returning next year. What a loss. Both are exceptional teachers.

Parent/guardian–teacher conferences are held from 1:00 to 6:00 p.m. Eleven out of 20 third graders had someone attend, and 30 of 44 fourth graders had a parent, aunt, or grandparent in attendance. With a few exceptions, those who came spoke of their support for the teachers and the school. At the other end of the building, the father of a kindergartener became loud and abusive toward a teacher. Ms. Dawson called the police.

Third Grade

Most parents/guardians at the conferences express concern about the state test that the fourth graders take. They ask if it is true that children who do well in their daily work and earn good grades can fail fourth grade if they fail the state test. The teacher tells them that this information is accurate. Sam's mother says, "Parents should get together and protest this test." They are told that that's probably the only way any change will occur.

Several mothers come to the conference wearing their fast-food uniforms. They have taken time off work to discuss their children's progress. One mother's breath smells strongly of an alcoholic beverage. She partially covers her mouth as she speaks. Another mother laments the absence of school prayer at Redbud Elementary.

A couple complains that not enough worksheets are sent home. They are given some suggestions about listening to and reading with their child every evening and perhaps taking him to the public library regularly. The teacher explains that scads of worksheets will not enrich their son's reading ability or interests. No parent or relative came for the seven poorest-performing children in the class.

Third and Fourth Grades

The day after conferences was called "teacher workshop." It was a day off for the children. This eagerly anticipated teacher workday turns out to be just that; however, it is filled with completing new forms, not working in their classrooms.

As the day begins, the intercom summons all teachers to the tiny office to pick up some "important" forms. On entering the office, teachers go through a large computer printout of every teacher in the district to locate their names and write "no" if they do not want their names given to telemarketers. No one writes "yes." Then names have to be located and addresses and phone numbers verified on the teacher roster. Next teachers are given their "professional growth folders."

In each folder is a four-page handout titled "A Guide to the Process of Meaningful Professional Growth Plans," written by a professor in Connecticut. It appears to have been taken from a textbook because of the page numbers (e.g., 199, 120) at the bottom of the handout pages.

There is no reference identifying the source of the handout. All questions are of the open-ended variety—not just checkoffs—for example, "List below two or three developments in your field that you need to become familiar with to be more current in your teaching. Identify an area where you are relatively weak and want to become more proficient. Identify an area that you could strengthen by working closely with a colleague."

The professor offers such advice as, "These professional growth plans are meaningful to the extent that they are based on worthwhile objectives. Sometimes teachers ask how do I get started on my objectives." (Few teachers—beginning or experienced—have heard a colleague ask, "How do I get started on my objectives?")

Another guideline stipulates, "First, a good objective is one that has an observable impact on the quality of the educational program in your school. Second, priority objectives should be important to you. They should give direction to your professional growth, excite your imagination, and provide a sense of satisfaction when achieved."

Next, teachers are to complete a district school board professional growth plan. This form requires the "evaluatee" and an "evaluator" to review performance objectives and professional plan activities four times during the year. A note at the bottom of the form states, "One objective per page; use additional sheet(s) if necessary."

When Pam Porter is asked about the purpose of completing these forms, she says, "The state auditor is coming in October and will audit these forms."

Intelligent educators often speak of the "state auditors" in somewhat hushed tones. University and public-school colleagues know that the amount of paperwork has increased enormously since the onset of the accountability movement. Every piece of paper, every form that someone completes, presumably, is subject to an audit. Educators relay that these audits occur and that the consequences of failure to complete the forms can be dire.

Later in the morning, grade-level teacher meetings are held. Each meeting is required to have a "recorder" whose job it is to complete a form that documents the meeting. The form contains the following elements: grade, date, presider, recorder, faculty/staff present, faculty/staff absent, topic of the meeting, and report of meeting. The veteran teachers say that every meeting has to be documented for the state. The third-grade meeting closes with Ms. Thibeaux's announcement that she has decided not to return to Redbud Elementary for a second year. She shakes her head and says, "This whole thing is crazy."

The afternoon begins with the discovery of a memo in mailboxes informing teachers that each of them will get $225 for supplies from the state. Attached to it is a form titled, "Guidelines for Purchasing Instructional Materials." Teachers' initial enthusiasm over the news that they will get some reimbursement is dampened when they read the guidelines, which include the following:

> The law requires that a minimum of 75 percent of these monies shall be used for teaching materials and supplies which are not consumed within a one-year period of time (examples include instructional software, software manuals, instruments, skeletal models, math manipulatives).
>
> The law also states that 25 percent of each allocation (i.e., $56.25) may be used for consumable-type instructional materials and supplies (e.g., paper, pencils, glue, chalk, markers, earth materials such as seeds).
>
> Please list what you buy on the attached form and keep all receipts.

This is the eighth week of school. Teachers have been buying items and saving receipts since the school year began. Few, if any, have bought such costly items as skeletal models. Teachers did not know that they would receive only twenty-five cents on the dollar for items such as paper and glue.

In other words, a teacher who bought stickers for 67 cents would compute the following: $.67 \times .25 = .1675$. This calculation would entitle the teacher, if the original receipt had been saved and attached to the form, to 17 cents (rounded up). What kind of mini-minded bureaucrat came up with this petty policy? And for such pathetic amounts! Most teachers have spent and will continue to spend many hundreds of dollars more, for which they will receive nothing.

Week 9, October 16–20: "We Could Wash Dogs"

Third and Fourth Grades

The teachers learn while on playground duty that a child has run away from her grandfather because he beats her with his fists. A meeting has been held in Pam Porter's office. The teachers also learn that a child in a third-grade class is being shuttled from relative to relative. He has no permanent home.

Both grade levels are discussing persuasive writing. The children write letters to the New Orleans Saints football team. Here are three of their unedited letters.

> Dear Saints,
> Our school has no playground equipment. Cold you send us some Narf footballs we wold like that. Maybe you can help redbud school out a littil.
>
> Your frind,
> Milo

> Dear New Orleans Saints,
> May you bring us some footballs, jump rops, soccer balls. When we go on the playground we don't have nothing to play with. We would be happy if we had something to play with.
>
> Your friend,
> LaDelle

> Dear New Orleans Saints,
> Our school has no playground equipment. Can you help us out we need so much. I'm in the fourth grade and I hope I pass the LEAP test. Will you guys pray for us? If you do, "thanks."
>
> Your friend,
> Carlonna

Third and Fourth Grades

The teachers arrive at 6:50 a.m. A thin woman with a black eye is waiting by the school office. The woman is dressed in a sleeveless white blouse and a straight skirt on this chilly morning. She is wearing sandals. The woman wants to enroll her daughter in preschool. The administrative assistant arrives as the teachers sign in for the day. The woman is told that there is no room at Redbud Elementary for the child. The preschool classes have reached their enrollment limit.

While on playground duty, Shenita points to a fourth-grade boy and says to the teachers, "Look at him. He's acting like a fool."

They respond, "He's twirling to show off for you."

Shenita replies with disgust, "He can twirl right on out of here." The teachers always enjoy talking with Shenita. She is a child who is wise beyond her years and has a quick wit. Her admirer is about half her size but persistent.

Fourth Grade

Each week, the students prepare for and look forward to their regular Friday event: reading to a class of third graders. In pairs, the fourth graders select a book, read it to the teacher, practice it at home, and then read the book to two or three third graders on Friday. When asked if this practice is worth continuing, the pupils assure their teacher that it is. "It helps us learn to read better," points out Jatoyia, "and it helps them learn to like books."

Graham adds, "We're helping them learn to read, too. They way behind."

After school, Pam Porter hands out two thick binders to each fourth-grade teacher, one binder containing state test materials for social studies and science, the other for English language and math. Each binder holds more than three hundred pages of information about the test's nature and type of questions, scoring procedures, and released test items from previous state tests.

A lot of the material prods teachers to teach to the test. What's missing is the most essential element: the materials to use with the children. For example, the social studies items contain a number of questions about federal and state governmental structures. The fourth-grade social studies text, however, focuses on the geographic regions of the United States.

Third Grade

Before teaching begins each day, teachers have numerous demands on their attention. For example, today Ms. Dawson tells the teacher, at 7:55 a.m., that the children weren't lining up fast enough to enter the building. Between 7:55 and 8:10 a.m., the following incidents take place:

- The teacher takes roll call and must record the absent children on a yellow slip of paper for the office and then note the absent children in her record book.
- Various monies must be collected. Today, money is brought in by two children for a play. The teacher must record the name of the child, the amount paid, and the date on a brown reservation form and write the same information on another sheet of paper.
- This sheet of paper goes into a tan money pouch, which must be sent to the office with the attendance slip.
- Three children have questions about work on the board (the district wants the children to be working immediately in the morning).
- Two children have lost their spelling lists and ask for replacements. The teacher makes a note to herself to copy two more lists.
- One child reports that he lost his math paper.

- A child finds another student's reading paper in his desk and tells this to the teacher.
- A pupil says that she cannot see the board. She is told to move her chair closer.
- Two children say they cannot find their pencils. Each is given a pencil with instructions to sharpen them.
- Jelani is tardy, not absent. This change must be made in the record book.
- A sheet comes from the grade-level representative. It is a reminder that progress reports are due next week. The teacher must get the report forms from the teachers' room and count out the correct number for the class.
- The children go to the restrooms. The physical education teacher and the third-grade teacher must supervise them.
- The administrative assistant is on the loudspeaker paging an adult.

It is 8:10, and the class says the Pledge of Allegiance.

The class is reading about a boy named Billy who rides his bike through a yellow light. A police officer is on the corner. Jimmy shouts out, "That is some dumb kid!" He shakes his head incredulously. Jimmy holds up his index finger and says, "First, Billy goes through the yellow light." Then Jimmy holds up a second finger and adds, "Second, he does this with a cop on the corner!" The entire class agrees that Billy isn't too bright.

Third and Fourth Grades

A team of experts from the governor's Office of Rural Development visited the town of Redbud to gather data. In their report, the team pointed out some contradictions. "The people are wonderful. It is a beautiful town. . . . Redbud has a jewel of a museum, a hidden treasure. . . . It is a great place, full of wonderful potential . . . but it was being undermined by poverty and drugs. . . . Drugs in Redbud are widespread and use is extremely high." The report noted that drugs are used by some children as young as 8. The drugs most commonly used are alcohol, marijuana, crack cocaine, prescription drugs, and methamphetamine.[1]

Fourth Grade

The week of October 23 has been designated Drug Awareness Week. Each fourth grader prepares an essay on the topic and draws a poster about drug awareness. LaDelle proudly displays her poster. On it are detailed illustrations and captions for each of the following: "bag of weed, 1/2 oz.; a joint (weed); lighter; crack cocaine (rock form); Premoe joint (half weed, half crack); crack cocaine pipe; elastic tie-off; cocaine cooking; drug needle and spoon; rolled up dollar bill; powder cocaine; razor blade table." The teacher wonders how many fourth graders in America possess this knowledge.

Third Grade

Today the teacher wants to explain types of maps to the children. She has several transparencies to show them. When she wants to use the overhead projector, she must first tighten a screw on the side of the mirror with a tiny Phillips screwdriver. Then she tapes paper to the blackboard because the classrooms have no screens and the images cannot be seen easily on the black surface of the board. The teacher becomes frustrated as the paper falls off the board. "I wish we had a screen," she says. "In my last classroom, I had a screen that I could pull down." She asks a rhetorical question: "Why do some schools have things and others don't?"

Manuel raises his hand. "Because the kids in other schools might work harder than we do," he offers.

"We work very hard," the teacher replies.

Shantel reports, "Some schools probably have rich principals, and they might give things to the teachers and the kids."

"We could write letters to rich schools and find out how they got all that stuff," suggests Haden.

Randall says, "Maybe we could trade some of our stuff with a rich school so we could get one of their screens."

"We could trade one of our air conditioners," Sam proposes. (The classroom has two tired, sputtering window air conditioners that spit out parts of their worn filters as they run.)

"Or we could trade Jesse's desk because he moved away," says Cherise. "Some schools might be too stingy, though, and want to keep all their screens."

"We could wash dogs to get money for a screen," suggests Randall.

"We'd have to wash a lot of dogs to buy a screen," the teacher replies. "We probably won't get a screen this year."

"That's okay," Kelvin adds consolingly. "All we need is each other."

Antinesha reports, "My cousin lives near Washington. His school has a stage and a lot of bathrooms. So the president probably decides who gets the money."

Randall nods and says, "I think that if you live close to the president, you get more money for your school. He can't send you a lot of money if you live far away like us because it might get lost in the mail." The other children nod in agreement.

Week 10, October 23–27: Another "New" Program

Third and Fourth Grades

The Monday faculty meeting begins at 3:00 p.m. sharp. Some of the teachers are speaking with the children who remain after the first buses leave. Ms. Dawson comes to find them. "You're late for the meeting," she says firmly.

Teachers write their names on the faculty sign-in sheet. Ms. Dawson is on a tear. At the meeting she tells the teachers that they are being too lax. "The children are not to fall asleep in class. If they do, stand them up! Don't let them wear coats in school. The children are using more time than is necessary getting in and out of the restrooms. We need to get test scores up, and you're using too much instructional time on this. Teachers, don't stand around talking the cafeteria. Stay on the children. There's too much talking. Teachers who can't do their job will be called in and talked to one-on-one."

After Ms. Dawson reprimands the teachers, they listen to a guest speaker, who talks about identifying homeless children. Then the featured attraction speaks—a consultant with the regional education agency. By now it is 3:45 p.m., and any hopes of getting away for a restroom break before the 5:00 PTO meeting begins are fading rapidly.

The consultant tells the teachers that they will be involved in a new endeavor: "whole-faculty study groups." They are handed an article to read and then divided into three groups. The consultant has marked where the ones, twos, and threes begin reading. Of course, the twos and threes have no notion of what precedes their sections without reading that material. What they are asked to read is out of context. She says, "This is the jigsaw method. You will each be an expert on your section."

The teachers begin reading the article. A snappy tune from the computer signals "time up" just as the twos and threes proceed to their portions of the article. "Now get together in groups. Make sure there are ones, twos, and threes in each group to talk about the article."

The author of the article seems to be writing in support of whole-faculty study groups. When the consultant is asked what research base supports using faculty time in this way, she replies, "They've been using it in St. Charles for 2 years, and their test scores are soaring." It doesn't seem to dawn on the consultant that these soaring scores could be attributed to dozens of things other than whole-faculty study groups, such as a library in the school, parents who can afford books, or different populations of children being tested during those 2 years.

Whole-faculty study groups choose something to study that will improve individual teaching and improve the school as a whole. Most teachers value the opportunity to share ideas with other teachers and always have done this. The "new" program formalizes a time-tested practice and destroys spontaneity. It requires each group member to serve a role and each group to keep a log (more paperwork and monitoring).

Math and technology apparently have been chosen by someone for Redbud Elementary. The consultant says that the students don't know math because the teachers "don't teach in-depth math like the Japanese and Germans do." She lectured, "They take about eight objectives and teach them deeply." The consultant seems to forget that the state math standards require that third-grade instructors, for example, teach 227 objectives. The state even tells the teachers which objectives must be covered in each 6-week period (e.g., 53 objectives must be covered in the first 6 weeks of school).

The consultant is asked where teachers, who have only 10 minutes a day free, will find time to participate in a whole-faculty study group. The consultant says with an unctuous smile, "Be creative! Don't worry—I'll be here to help you. I can come every Monday for an after-school meeting."

The teachers at Redbud Elementary School are the experts. They know their pupils, they know the community, and they know the needs. They do not need consultants to tell them what to do. But no one in the state or in the district ever seems to ask the teachers how to make things better.

After the meeting with the regional consultant, teachers must again sign in—this time for the PTO meeting. As they take their seats before Pam Porter begins, a competent first-grade teacher announces that she will not be returning to Redbud Elementary next year. "I just want to teach. I can't do that here with all these add-ons," she says. Another teacher chimes in, "This whole-faculty study group thing may be the add-on that pushes me over the edge."

Fourth Grade

Mrs. Redd is helping the fourth-grade students learn to use the $85,500 assessment program. She has completed the time-consuming task of entering all the children into both the assessment and instructional programs. The program is slow, and the students often have to wait for a screen to change.

Sometimes they impatiently click the "enter" key more than once. When they do, nothing moves. Mrs. Redd cautions, "The pretest has two parts. Part 1 has 57 questions, and part 2 has 71 questions. You must be careful. Say you're on question 56 and you tap 'enter' twice. It will freeze and you'll have to log out, log on, and start over." Teachers wonder how much of a time-wasting boondoggle this large investment will be.

Third and Fourth Grades

A traveling children's theater group will present *Aladdin and the Magic Lamp* at Redbud High School, which is a block from Redbud Elementary. Wednesday morning from 10:30 to 11:30 is reserved for the performance.

Each pupil must pay $2.50 to attend. The day before the performance, more than half the children have been unable to come up with the amount.

Most teachers pull out their wallets so that their students do not have to stay behind and work while the children who had $2.50 walk excitedly to the high school. Something is terribly wrong when a school district spends $85,500 on a computer program to prepare children for a high-stakes test but won't spend a comparatively measly sum to send economically disadvantaged children to a play.

Third Grade

The teacher finds a rotten little tooth on the classroom floor. "Who lost a tooth?" she asks. The children search their mouths with their tongues. Kanzah comes up to the teacher and retrieves the tooth. There are no tooth fairies in Redbud.

NOTE

1. Susan T. Herring, "Governor's Resource Team Impressed by Redbud's Beauty," *Guardian-Journal*, October 19, 2000, 1, 5.

Chapter Four

Drugs, Poverty, and Test Scores

November, December

Week 11, October 30–November 3: "It Just Hurts My Heart"

Fourth Grade

Two essays (both edited for spelling) from the Drug Awareness Week contest were not selected as winners last week, but they are poignant testimonials to the impact of drugs on the pupils. Malcolm wrote:

> Drugs are everywhere. I see people walking down the street acting like something wrong. They come over the fence in the backyard when we are not home and steal things from our backyard. They steal our hanging plants late at night. They come to our house trying to sell us things that they might have taken from someone else. They seem like they do not eat any food from looking at their size, sometimes they ask if we have something for them to do to get money, and seem like they never go home at all.

Emerald wrote:

> Drugs affect my family my dad do all kinds of drugs. He do dope and weed. My uncle do weed. It just hurts my heart. I feel like one day they going to get the wrong thing. When my dad had smoke weed he tried to burn down my grandmother's house. I was crying when my dad tried to burn up my grandmother's house and he live there.

Third Grade

The teacher learns a new word from her third graders: *blackmoll*. They, too, ask to make drug awareness posters as the fourth graders have. One poster has a bottle drawn and labeled "gine" (gin) on it. Jelani asks how to spell *blackmoll*.

"What's that?" the teacher asks.

She hears many voices and calls on Haden. "It's like a cigar, but the stuff inside has been scraped out and weed is put in. It's got a white plastic tip on the end. The teacher spells the word the best she can.

Kanzah is absent this morning. "Where is Kanzah?" the teacher inquires.

Antinesha says, "He probably won't come because his mother got put in jail last night. She was fighting and the policemens came and the ambulance came."

"I saw it," adds Wendice. "They was cut and bleeding and one had a knot on her head." He points to his forehead.

Fourth Grade

The teacher continues to be struck by the generosity of the children who live in poverty. When Dario or Victavius can't find their pencils, several students offer to let the boys borrow one. The same is true with notebook paper. Today Joshua, Jamal, and Dwayne bring their bulging bags of trick-or-treat candy to share with the class during snack time. Perhaps, for these children, it is the only way of ever treating the class because they have so little.

Third and Fourth Grades

This is the week of the all-school book fair. On the first day, children are allowed, by classes, to go into the gym and browse among the books and toys for sale. On the remaining days, only children who have money to buy books are allowed into the gym at their scheduled time.

Each class can remain in the gym for 15 minutes the first day. The children see many books they would like to own but cannot.

The computer lab is closed all week. Mrs. Redd, the paraprofessional who runs the lab, has been assigned to work at the book fair this week—even though most of the children cannot afford to purchase books.

Fourth Grade

The teacher is concerned about Rachael, who just transferred to Redbud Elementary. In her first week, she already has been in one playground fight. Today she was sent to in-school suspension by Ms. Dawson for saying unkind things to Chalese, a shy child who has learning disabilities. Rachael is the fifth child who has enrolled in the classroom since the school year began. The teacher knows that with each new face, the chemistry of the class changes.

Third Grade

The third graders accurately reported the incident involving Kanzah's mother. Her name is in the arrest section of the Redbud weekly newspaper. Bond is set at $1,500.

Week 12, November 6–10: Prior Knowledge

Third and Fourth Grades

It is the twelfth week of school, and many of the fourth graders have not yet been able to complete the assessment program and enter the instructional program of the new $85,500 software package that is supposed to "pinpoint" difficulties. The rest of the school cannot use the computer lab because it is reserved for the fourth graders, who go there twice a day for half an hour—once for reading and once for math. The only time the other children get a glimpse of the computer lab is when they walk past it on their way to the portable music classroom.

Third Grade

The children take care of one another. On Tie Day, Redbud Elementary students are allowed to wear men's ties. Chikae brings a tie, but he doesn't know how to tie it. Antinesha ties it for him in a perfect knot. Where did she learn this? Jaheesa's braids are too tight. Shantel takes off Jaheesa's hair bows (barrettes) and loosens Jaheesa's braids. Cherise's ear is bleeding from a too-big earring in her pierced ear. Kanesha removes the earring and gets Cherise a wet paper towel to place on the ear. All of this is accomplished without directions from the teacher. The children frequently exhibit compassion and unselfishness.

The pupils' lack of prior knowledge, at least the type that appears on many standardized tests, is apparent daily. On a test provided by the balanced literacy series that the school is using, all the children incorrectly complete an item. They can pronounce the word *harp*, but they have no idea of what the words means. The class looks up *harp* in a dictionary and are fortunate that an illustration accompanies the definition.

In a balanced literacy book selection, the word *recital* is part of the book's title and central to the plot of the story. No child in the class ever has taken a music lesson or a dance lesson, and no child has ever attended a recital. In the language books, the word *opera* appears in an exercise. Again, no child knows the meaning.

Today the class teaches their teacher a meaning for the word *poor*. The subject of discussion is healthy and unhealthy foods. Antinesha comments, "My cousin eats a lot but he's still *poe*."

"What's *poe*?" the teacher asks.

"You know like when somebody doesn't have money but this means somebody's skinny," Antinesah replies.

"Oh, *poor*," the teacher says. "I never heard of that meaning of the word." She looks it up in a large dictionary that she brought from home. The children are correct. A meaning of *poor* is *emaciated*. "You taught me something new," the teacher tells them.

Leon proudly shows the teacher his new shoes from Wal-Mart: white tennis shoes that are too big. After recess she sees him wiping dust off them with a dry paper towel. She tells him that he is smart to take such good care of his new shoes.

Some of the students can tell time, and others cannot. The teacher has those who know how to tell time help those who are having some problems. As she walks around the room offering assistance, she notices that the tutors have drawn lopsided clocks and are showing their tutees how to count by fives and ones to determine the correct time. The tutors are patient with their pupils. The teacher thinks that sometimes the children offer better explanations of things to other children than she can.

The teacher brings in a lamp for the children's "library time." Twenty minutes before the children go home each day, she will turn off the overhead lights and turn on the new lamp. Pupils have signed up to read a picture book to the class during this time. Even the children who read below grade level want to take a turn. Manuel bumps the new lamp on the way to the pencil sharpener. "Be careful!" Shantel says to Manuel. "There's no money-back guarantee on lamps."

Jelani and Kanzah ask to get water several times today. Their gums are bleeding. The teacher reminds them to tell their grandmothers because they live with them.

The class is given their final test in carrying and regrouping (borrowing). Each child is called to the teacher's desk to discuss errors and get some extra help where needed. Wendice does poorly on the borrowing section, missing most of the problems. He is asked if his mother can help him a bit at home. "No," he replies. "When I get home, she drunk."

"Every day?" the teacher inquires.

"Every day she drunk or gone." The teacher tells Wendice that they'll find a helper at school.

When the teacher asks Ms. Dawson about Wendice's home life, Ms. Dawson says that the mother was a "dopehead" and still is "a drunk." The teacher is told, "You'll get no help from there."

Week 13, November 13–17: "Drink a Beer"

Third Grade

While reviewing the vowel team *oa*, the teacher learns another meaning of the word *roast* from the third graders. Leon explains, "When you get *roast*, you get hit with a big, wide, thick strap."

"You have to get hit until you get bruises to get *roast*," Shantel points out. The other children agree.

Third and Fourth Grades

Pam Porter sends a letter and a copy of the school report card for parents home with the children. The report card shows that Redbud Elementary has dropped from a school performance score of 44.1 to 41.3. This score labels the school "academically below average." In her letter to parents and guardians, Pam explains that the low score was based on tests given last March and did not include the state test scores of students who attended summer school and then passed their retakes of the test. She also points out that school attendance accounts for 10% of the total school score, and she urges parents and guardians to keep their children's attendance high.

The teachers wonder why school officials and politicians across the country seem oblivious to or disinterested in the omnipresent correlation between children living in poverty and low test scores. They are not making excuses—they are stating a fact. In the state, schools that score at the bottom are in the high-poverty areas. The schools that score at the top are the magnet schools and campus lab schools with selective admissions procedures. Other schools performing well are found in areas of affluence. Furthermore, many parents, particularly White parents with the means to do so, send their children to private academies and Christian schools.

Third Grade

This morning, the 8-year-olds are filled with etymological and medical knowledge and social advice. Kanzah announces that he has diarrhea and must go to the bathroom frequently. The teacher tells the class that this condition can be dangerous because it can cause dehydration. They need to drink fluids if they have it. "It's bad. You can die from it," Manuel says seriously. "That's why they call it *die*-arrhea." The class nods with looks of "I haven't thought about this, but it makes sense."

The discussion turns to ringworm. Nearly every child in the class has had ringworm, and they offer the same medical advice: "Drink a beer."

"When I had it bad," Keaziah tells us, "my mama gave me Bud Light and it went away fast." Other children offer similar testimonials.

Cherise asks the teacher if she knows how to tell when somebody is growing.

"By measuring them?" the teacher offers.

"No, you can tell when you're growing because there's a hole in the back of your knee, and when that hurts, you're growing," she says confidently.

"I wet the bed sometimes," reports Jaron.

Shantel gives him a disapproving look. "If I did that, I'd keep it to myself," she says.

After lunch, the teacher walks into the gym early to pick up her class. They are trying to make baskets in the one hoop near the main doors. She realizes the importance of seeing the whole child—creating, at work, and at play. Wendice, who often is lethargic because of the late hours he keeps, is a whiz on the court. Wendice is tiny for his age. He comes up to the teacher with the comparatively huge basketball, smiles, and says, "This one's for you."

Then he dribbles, aims, and, with all his strength, hurls the basketball. He makes a basket.

Third and Fourth Grades

Friday is here, and the dismissal bell rings. Next week is the Thanksgiving holiday. Several of the children linger in classrooms, pretending to be busy. Some tell their teachers that they do not want to go home. After the children finally leave, Ruth says that this behavior is not uncommon. "They get two meals a day here, they have a schedule, they're safe, and they have people who care. They know they won't get this at home."

Week 14, November 27–December 1: Teachers *Will* Be Held Accountable

Fourth Grade

The week begins with an announcement by Nikeya that there is a cockroach on De'Lewis's book bag. De'Lewis jumps up and swats at it. Jamal leaps out of his chair saying, "I'll get it," and he squashes the roach.

Yolande has not come to school for more than 8 weeks. At first it was rumored that she was moving; however, she is truant. Each day, students report that Yolande is still in Redbud. The teacher has reported this every morning on the attendance slip. According to school records, Yolande missed 62 days last year. The principal notified the truant officer and social services, but nothing seems to bring her back to school. Today, Jaylene announces, "Yolande said she's coming back to class on Monday."

Third Grade

The teacher is on playground duty at 7:15 a.m. When the bell rings, Mrs. Marlow tells her that office personnel have been paging the teacher repeatedly. She ushers her class into their classroom, and coat still on, she hurries to the office. A grandmother and a third grader carrying a Wal-Mart bag of school supplies await her. The teacher greets the child, speaks briefly with the grandmother, and escorts the child to the classroom.

Ms. Tompkins, an in-school suspension substitute, is waiting for the teacher by the classroom door. She reprimands the teacher, in front of the class, about the children's behavior while the teacher was in the office. The teacher puts wadded paper towels under a leg of a desk to balance it for the new child and takes roll call. Then she takes off her coat.

Fourth Grade

Two pupils are sick today. Rhonda tells the teacher about her stomachache as the tears roll. Dwayne, his hat pulled far over his head, slumps with a severe headache. Telephone calls to both homes yield no results. Rhonda's mother says that she cannot leave her small child, so Rhonda will just have to stay at school. Dwayne's mother cannot be reached. There is no place in the school where sick children can lie down.

Third and Fourth Grades

Teachers learn that the school was broken into during the Thanksgiving vacation. The vandals stood on a garbage can and broke into a window in a restroom. Pam Porter says that the damage was minor. Salt was poured on the floors, paint was sprayed in a restroom, small items were tossed about, and decorations and students' work were torn from the walls.

Third Grade

The temperature is in the 30s when the children arrive today. Some of them are dressed in short-sleeved shirts and shorts. They are not wearing sweaters or jackets, and they shiver in the cold. As the teacher opens her classroom door, she sees a mess. The vandals have struck again. This time they hit the rooms that had been used for tutoring children after school.

These rooms were not locked when the tutoring sessions were dismissed. The contents of the teacher's desk are scattered on the floor. She had a few dollars in her desk to supply children with loans. This money is missing. Other teachers find that contents of their desks and files are scattered about.

After the 10-minute morning recess, Gerard tells the teacher that he wants to speak to her privately. The three other children standing near her go to their desks. "What's the problem?" she asks.

"Two boys on the playground are calling me 'Chubs' and 'Pork Chop.'"

"That's terrible," the teacher says. "Who are these boys?"

"I don't know their names. But that's not all," Gerard continues. "They said, 'If you eat another crumb, you'll explode.'"

"You'll have to point them out to me the next time we have recess," she says.

"I'm going to set a trap for them," confides Gerard. "I'll take my trading cards with me, and when they see me playing with them, they'll come near me, and then I can show you who they are."

"That's a fine plan," the teacher responds.

Fourth Grade

Today student teachers arrive. They will be with the third- and fourth-grade classes until February 22. The university that they attend is on the quarter system. Ms. Hammond is from a nearby town. The students seem pleased to have her in the room. Demetrius guesses her age to be 14; she is 23.

Third Grade

The regular, cooperating teacher knows her student teacher, Ms. Melody Schwartz, because Ms. Schwartz was a student in the "Diagnosing Reading Difficulties" course that the teacher taught last year. Ms. Schwartz is told the daily routine and is given the few teachers' manuals that are available. Ms. Schwartz has the enthusiasm that the teacher frequently sees in those just beginning their careers.

The students in the class and in the fourth-grade class show off for the student teachers. Jimmy tells Ms. Schwartz, "They're acting like a bunch of wild animals." The experienced teachers know that this behavior will diminish as the children become accustomed to the student teachers' presence in the rooms.

Week 15, December 4–8: "Things in My Life Goes Bad"

Fourth Grade

The day begins by having the students to write a two-paragraph description of the highlights of their weekend. Emerald's (unedited) is particularly tragic:

> My House Fire
>
> Thing that happened in my life is that my house got burn up. got burn up. First it starting at the top and then it just starting to burn. My close, shoes, and bed, toys and my fish tank. It is sad because my brothers game got burn up. One

thing about is that everybody come to help my mom. My grandmother tried to run back in there but my mom hold my grandmother back.

In my life at my uncle house has been so bad. My cousin always picking on me and they don't like me. My uncle try to make me happy but he cannot make me happy. Things in my life goes bad.

Third and Fourth Grades

On Monday morning, the announcement is made that all teachers are to turn in their lesson plan books and grade books to the office immediately. Late in the day, the books are returned to the teachers by the grade-level representatives. Several plan books contain sticky notes that point out deficiencies. Presumably the inspection was conducted by Pam Porter, but it is not made clear who insisted on the inspection and why.

There were two more break-ins this week. On Monday night, a window in Mr. Effingham's room was broken, and things were scattered about. The entry point of the most recent break-in has not been discovered. Some sort of alarm system is being installed. Several teachers have expressed fears about staying in the building after dark. "I don't want to be here when somebody's creeping around," commented Ms. Larson.

Teachers receive a memo from Pam Porter stating, among other things, that there will be faculty meetings the next two Monday evenings. Consultants will be at the school to model whole-faculty study groups. Teachers have no voice in this matter.

Fourth Grade

The commercial photographers are back to take holiday pictures of those who can afford the $10–$40 package. Only a few students in each class bring the minimum amount of money. They are allowed to wear "dress-up clothes" rather than school uniforms. Birdia, who is in Ruth's fourth-grade class, comes to school in a baby-blue, frilly, taffeta-like dress. When the teachers tell her how beautiful she looks, she says, "I got it for Easter. My grandpa told me he will bring the picture money later." Ruth says that it is unlikely that the grandfather will appear. The grandfather never does come to school with the picture money.

On picture days the new teachers see the benefits of school uniforms. When the children wear their "very best," they see baggy men's shirts and pants and men's ties on the boys and ill-fitting, hand-me-down, well-worn party dresses on the girls. The clothing jars the new recruits and reminds them how little their pupils have in terms of material goods. The children are not aware of their poverty now as they move about the room in their finest attire, but they will be as the years pass.

Ruth paid for Birdia's photograph. The new teachers continue to be struck by the generosity and big hearts of some of the teachers at Redbud Elementary, who are among the most poorly paid teachers in the United States. They buy school supplies, pay for theatrical productions, and buy treats; most of all, they give a lot of love to the children.

Third and Fourth Grades

Another warning came today from Ms. Dawson. Teachers are told to "clamp down" on talking in the lunchroom. "Too many teachers are talking to each other when they should be monitoring their students." Teachers who fail to comply are to be "talked to individually."

The area has been experiencing a cold snap this week. Every night, the temperature dips below 30 degrees. Children sit in the hallways after breakfast instead of playing outside before school starts. Some do not wear sweaters or jackets.

The weather is too much for the air conditioners/heaters in the classrooms. They freeze up, make clunking noises, and kick out no heat. The custodians have to be called several times to get them working again. Classrooms are chilly most of the week because these window units are not airtight. Large gaps offer a good view of the schoolyard from the fourth-grade room and views of the driveway from the third-grade classroom. A small bird could easily hop through the gaps.

"A fungus known as 'stachybotrys' was found in several rooms of at Redbud Memorial Hospital about a month ago, causing hospital officials to close down one wing of the hospital."[1] Hospital employees had complained because of illness. At Redbud Elementary School, children and teachers take turns having viral infections, skin rashes, and more. Teachers suspect something lurks in the damp, moldy ceiling tiles in their classrooms.

Week 16, December 11–15: Teaching and Learning in a Cold Building

Third and Fourth Grades

The teachers arrive at school to find that there has been a power outage. The classrooms have no heat or lights. The air temperature is 27 degrees; strong winds have snapped power lines. At 7:55, teachers begin to conduct classes in cold, dark classrooms. Children who have coats keep them on; a few unclaimed sweaters and jackets from years past are distributed to children who are wearing only short-sleeved shirts.

When the power is restored at approximately 9:30, the window heaters begin to chug. They kick out air—first cool, then tepid, then warm. The rooms on the sunny side of the building begin to warm up. Those on the shady side are cold all day.

Third Grade

Kanzah brings aspirin to school. In the morning, he asks the teacher if he can take a tablet because he has a toothache. She asks him if he has gone to a dentist as his grandmother said he would. "No," he says.

Wendice is crying with tooth pain. The teacher sends him to the office to call his mother. She picks him up. The next morning, the teacher asks him if he has seen a dentist. "No," he replies.

Fourth Grade

Room H gets so cold that the teacher visits Wal-Mart and purchases two electric heaters. He hopes that they will provide enough heat to supplement the inadequate window units.

The next morning, the teacher plugs in the heaters and immediately blows a fuse. He learns that he will be able to plug in one heater if no computers are in use and nothing else is plugged in. Children and teachers have gotten used to wearing coats and gloves in class.

Third Grade

Jaheesa is having problems listening in class. She writes the following apology (edited for spelling) to her teachers:

> I will not talk on the rug or at my desk. I know I talk but I just can't help myself. I know they say zip your lips and throw away the key. I tried that but it didn't help and they say put your hand on your mouth. But that did not help.
>
> Today is my birthday and God knows I do not want to act like this. When I am at home I will talk and my dad says I talk too much. He said if I get a letter from your teachers he said they are not lying because you talk too much at home. I wish I can stop talking. I am sorry that I was talking on the rug.

Gerard comes up to the teacher's desk. He looks pale and asks if he can go to the restroom. When he returns, he raises his hand. "Can I tell you something?" he asks.

"Sure," the teacher responds.

He comes up to her desk. "I barfed," he whispers.

"Do you want to go home?" she asks.

"There is a good thing and a bad thing if I go home," Gerard states.

"What are those things?" the teacher inquires.

"The good thing is that if I barf again, I'll be at home. The bad thing is that I'll miss my studies."

"I think you had better go home," she tells him. "I'll get your schoolwork together for you, and you can do it if you feel better later."

Gerard goes to the office to call his grandmother to pick him up.

Week 17, December 18–19: Still No Heat

Fourth Grade

There are only one and a half days this week because of winter vacation. It's a good thing because the fourth-grade classroom has no heat, and the temperature outside each morning has been below freezing. One window heater does not turn on at all, and the other blows cool air. It is difficult to learn in the cold.

Tuesday morning is devoted to room holiday parties, so the teacher takes his fourth graders, carrying their desk chairs, to a somewhat-warm third-grade classroom for a joint party. He decides that if the heaters are not fixed by the time school resumes on January 2, he will ask Pam Porter to find space for his students in the cafeteria or the gymnasium.

NOTE

1. Susan T. Herring, "Stachybotrys Fungus Found at Redbud Memorial Hospital Has Been Removed," *Guardian-Journal*, December 7, 2000, 1.

Chapter Five

Test Preparation, the Pace Quickens

January, February

Week 18, January 2–5: School of Academic Distinction

Third Grade

When the teacher is in her classroom before school begins, the evening custodian appears. For weeks, he has swept around a desk that is somewhat leveled by two ancient language arts textbooks propped under a short desk leg. She has sent notes to the office (following the correct procedure for reporting repairs) to no avail. The teacher asks the custodian to fix the leg of the desk. He does so in less than a minute. His shoes stick to the floor of the classroom just as hers do. The promised winter-break mopping of the filthy classroom floors never took place.

Fourth Grade

Room H still has no heat. The window heater does not work at all, and the other continues to blow only cold air. The teacher asks Pam Porter if anything can be done to repair or replace the heaters. The temperature in the room is not above 20 degrees. Later Pam informs him via the intercom that someone will come to replace a heater. The children and the teacher wear coats, hats, and gloves, but it is not possible to concentrate on teaching and learning. Many of the children are ill dressed for such temperatures.

    The pupils become a class of vagabonds seeking heat. They spend an hour working in a third-grade classroom and some time in the computer lab, which has a little heat. On the way to the lab, they notice that Ms. Marlow has her third-grade class in the gym. She is trying to teach a lesson while another class is involved in a noisy basketball game. Later, Room H's class spends time watching educational videos in Ruth Waverly's room.

By midday, a new window heater has been installed, but it has insufficient power to make a dent in the cold air. It is meant for a tiny office. A man inspects the heater that blows cold air and gives Room H's teacher the impression that something will be done. At the end of the school day, the room is still frigid.

Third and Fourth Grades

The teachers note that the New Orleans Saints are going to face the Minnesota Vikings in a second-round playoff game. The children never heard from the Saints in response to their letters and the teachers' letter describing the lack of playground equipment. The pupils have given up asking about the letters.

Third Grade

Today is Jelani's birthday. "My daddy is wearing an alarm on his leg," he says, "but he's gonna take it off."

"Why is he going to take it off?" the teacher asks.

"So he can come to see me for my birthday," Jelani answers.

Fourth Grade

Room H is warm. The teacher left the new heater on overnight, and the temperature has climbed into the 50s. The pupils can stay in their room today.

Rhonda asks if she can talk with the teacher. "Sure," the teacher says.

"Have I been better?" she asks. "Have I been talking less? I'm on a new medication. Sometimes my mama loses patience with me. My brother is the same way. Mama divorced my dad because he was doing so much drugs. My aunt said if mama had stayed married to him, we wouldn't have anything—not even a house. We would be on the street."

"Where is your dad now?" the teacher inquires.

Rhonda responds, "Oh, he's around. He doesn't really live anywhere. I might not be in school on Monday because he might take me to Monroe or Shreveport just so we can have a day together." "No problem. I hope you have a great time," the teacher comments.

"Well, it might not happen," she says.

Week 19, January 8–12: "But Everybody Likes Each Other"

Third Grade

Jelani's father did not cross state lines to attend his son's birthday celebration.

Roland comes up to the teacher's desk. "I went in my pants," he whispers.

"Do you want to call your mother?" the teacher asks.

"Yes, but I can't go home because if I don't have perfect attendance, I can't get the money at the end of the year."

Roland's mother arrives with a change of pants for him. He stays in school the rest of the day. He is too ill to work and sleeps at his desk.

Fourth Grade

Emerald asks to speak with the teacher. "I saw my daddy this weekend. He at Warton."

"Oh, I hear that Warton is pretty nice," says the teacher.

Emerald continues, "He don't work there. He in there. He didn't pay child support to my mama. He gave me a letter, and I have it in my folder. Do you want to see it?"

"Sure, if you want me to," the teacher answers.

The letter is two pages in length and gives evidence of a writer who is barely literate. He tells about incidents at Warton, tells Emerald how much he loves her, and promises that things will be different when he gets out. Emerald, her mother, and three brothers are still living with an uncle's family because the trailer they bought after their house fire is not yet ready for occupancy.

Rhonda informs the teacher that her dad didn't show up to take her to Monroe or Shreveport for the father-daughter day they had planned. "I suppose he got tied up. But I had fun at my aunt's house," Rhonda says.

Next Monday is Dr. Martin Luther King Jr. Day. There will be no school. Teachers read a picture book about Dr. King's life to their classes.

"Why did they kill him?" asks Tyler. "He was for peace and love."

Verlin says, "Here's one good thing: We're different colors in this class, but everybody likes each other. That's what Dr. King wanted."

Week 20, January 16–19: Preparing for High-Stakes Tests

Third Grade

The class is reading a story in the balanced literacy series about a family (father, mother, and child) who arrive at an airport, check in, and proceed to the departure gates. "How many of you have been to an airport?" the teacher inquires. Three students raise their hands.

"My stepdad took me on an airplane," says Jaron. "They sold hot dogs at the airport."

"I was on an airplane when I was little," adds Shantel. "I don't remember it, and it's a good thing, too. I'm afraid of heights."

"I kinda was at an airport," offers Manuel. "We drove past one once."

The pupils, except for one, have no prior knowledge of baggage tags, check-in procedures, security measures, airport design, "tugs" that push planes back, or in-flight and landing procedures.

Fourth Grade

The class roster continues to change. LaTonya, Danika, and Kamie are gone, and soon Malcolm will leave.

Today is report card day. Yolande is not present. Her report card shows that she has missed 48 days of school. She isn't ill; she just isn't coming to school. The teacher has phoned Yolande's grandmother, and so has Ms. Dawson. The absences have been reported to the truancy officer. Yolande had the same high absentee rate in third grade and had to repeat the grade. No sensible person could hold teachers accountable for something out of their control, but that's exactly what some aspects of accountability do. Absentee rates are figured into a school score and reported on a school report card.

Third and Fourth Grades

The new teachers are becoming immune to the filth in which they work. The student teachers frequently comment on the condition of the building. Ms. Hammond says, "I could never teach in this dirty school."

Classroom floors go unmopped and sometimes unswept. It is not uncommon to see a teacher pushing a broom or squatting to scrub a section of the floor. The school has three custodians who double as bus drivers and cafeteria workers. One reportedly also works as an orderly at the Redbud hospital.

Third Grade

Haden has a headache, but despite the throbbing, he cannot stay awake. "Do you want to call home?" the teacher asks.

"I can't. They're at work."

"Can you call someone at work to pick you up? You seem very sick."

"I am sick, but I'm not supposed to call anybody," he murmurs.

The new teacher asks another teacher why some parents or guardians would want a sick child to sit at his or her desk all day rather than be home in bed.

"It's poverty" is the answer from the Redbud veteran. "The parent can't afford to lose a day's pay or can't afford a babysitter, so the child sits in school."

In connection with some social studies lessons, the student teacher, Ms. Schwartz, wants to take the children to the local Dodge Museum for a field trip. The cost is 50 cents per child. Gerard becomes upset.

"I can't go," he cries. "I'm not smart and so I won't get a good report card and then I won't get the 50 cents."

Immediately Jaheesa tells Gerard that she has 50 cents he can have. Jimmy assures Gerard that he, too, has 50 cents at home and will bring it so Gerard can go on the field trip with the class.

The realities of high-stakes testing hit home today for the children and their teachers. A section of a practice standardized reading test is given. The children have 45 minutes to read six selections and answer 20 questions. The items are designed to test skills such as main idea/details, sequence, cause and effect, character analysis, and so on.

The test results are miserable. Only six children "pass" the test. If this had been the high-stakes state test after summer remediation, 14 of the children in the class would have had to repeat the grade. The most surprising thing about the results is that three of the top readers did not pass. They are among the few who read at grade level. And the practice test is for second grade—not third grade.

The teachers try to figure out what happened. Antinesha says that she did poorly because she had to take care of her baby sister all night. "I have to change her and feed her," the third-grader reports. Other children misnumber many of their answers and therefore score low. Most of the children lack the prior knowledge to fully comprehend the selections. Several of the special education children who take the test lack the skills to complete even one section.

Some of the children were staring into space during the testing time, preoccupied with childhood daydreams or more serious thoughts. It is difficult to convince children that high-stakes tests can alter their lives when many still believe in Santa Claus.

Week 21, January 22–26: "Stay Away From Crackheads"

Third and Fourth Grades

A 5:30 a.m. local television show features a school that has won a School Spirit Award. Scores of happy-appearing, jumping, shouting White children are in the school gym. They are waving large, oblong balloons. The school principal is interviewed. He exudes pride about the School Spirit Award and comments on achieving the School of Academic Distinction ranking. He points out that his school is in the top 1% of all the schools in the entire state.

The camera scans the school playground, which is equipped with all the latest play structures. Inside the school building, the viewer is shown eager-looking children reading books. The principal praises their "great PTO," which just had a fund-raiser and bought a new state-of-the-art playground structure for the children to use at recess.

The teachers know this school. It is somewhat new and well maintained, and it serves a neighborhood of subdivisions with expensive homes. One of the teachers there notes that the principal likes to brag about the school being a neighborhood school—not a magnet school like other schools of academic distinction. "But look at the neighborhood. Look at the beautiful homes. We should be a school of distinction. The children have everything at home," she points out.

It is apparent to all American teachers that schools serving children of affluence, with few exceptions, have a much easier job than schools serving children of poverty. It is the schools of affluence that usually have the highest test scores, get the highest rankings, and receive kudos in local newspapers. They get all the goodies.

Third Grade

This same morning as the new teachers drive toward school, they notice that Jaheesa is not standing at her usual bus spot on Dr. Martin Luther King Jr. Street. Instead, she stands two blocks further on. In science class, the third graders are talking about movement of seeds, animals (i.e., migration), and humans. Modes of transportation are discussed (e.g., train travel). Wendice says, "I walk along the train tracks and see crackheads." The teacher tells him that walking along train tracks is dangerous and that he should cease the practice.

"Stay away from crackheads, too," she adds. "They can do bad things to people."

"Somebody killed a woman last night," says Jaheesa, "right by where I live." A roomful of hands go up. Most of the children have heard about the murder. "The killer did this," Jaheesa reports. She draws her finger from one ear, across her throat, to the other ear.

The brutally murdered woman was 49 years old. A local television station interviewed the victim's neighbors, who exhibited fear because the murderer had not been apprehended. One neighbor told the reporter, "What scares us is that it is somebody among us." The pupils at Redbud Elementary School always have much more on their minds and in their lives than academic skills. The murdered woman is the grandmother of a child in the third-grade class, Room B.

Fourth Grade

The state test frenzy is increasing. Every teacher gets a memorandum that reads,

> The State Department of Education is providing all schools a grant for remediation of all fourth grade students. They will pay teachers and/or tutors to teach students in a ratio of 5:1, and will provide a scripted guide and all materials. This is the first time any guide has been provided that is consistent with the LEAP test.
>
> As you can see with this ratio of five students to one teacher, we will need at least eighteen teachers/tutors at this school alone. We are planning on holding these classes on Monday and Wednesday since the Title I classes are already on Tuesday and Thursday. This will give fourth graders an opportunity to attend all sessions.
>
> Those working in this program will be paid by the hour an amount determined by the central office. If you will teach in this program let me know IMMEDIATELY since we must start as soon as we are able. This will continue until the week before the LEAP tests.

Students eligible for this new tutoring program are those who scored below the 31st percentile on the third-grade Iowa test. That totals more than 90 of the 120 fourth-grade students at Redbud Elementary.

The $85,500 computer program that was going to "pinpoint" and "remediate" the skill needs of these same fourth graders is a lemon. Half the time the program doesn't work at all, and when it does work, it is a painfully slow collection of drill-and-practice routines. The fourth-grade teachers now skip most of their assigned computer times.

Fourth-grade teachers are given a stack of 94-page Iowa test practice booklets to use with their students before the March 12 state test begins. To do so would consume dozens of hours of instructional time. Why are fourth graders being asked to practice for the Iowa test when they will be taking the state test? The school's name should be changed to Redbud Test Preparation Center so that it more accurately depicts what goes on inside its walls.

Third and Fourth Grades

The teachers receive a memo from the central office informing them of procedures to follow if they want to recommend students for art instruction. The form includes the following seven evaluative statements about a student being considered for art class:

Draws more than his/her peers.
Draws better than his/her peers.
Volunteers to do art or art-like activities.
Deferred to by other students when drawing or making objects.

Brings drawings or art made at home to school.
Sets high standards of quality for his/her artwork.
Reacts with interest and excitement to art activities and information.

Each statement is rated from 1 (seldom or never) to 5 (almost always). A statement that receives a score of 4 or 5 must be supported by two examples of the student's work, two statements of support (presumably written by the teacher), or one statement and one example. "In other words, when you are finished, there must be a TOTAL of 14 examples and statements. HINT: They will not accept drawings of cartoon characters such as Mickey Mouse, Donald Duck, or Pokemon, etc." The memo points out that a student must have a score of 34 or 35 to "continue to the next level."

The teachers would like to recommend all their students for art. The children need aesthetic experiences and outlets for their creativity. To recommend the 66 students in the combined classes of Rooms B and H would require writing 924 statements or assembling 924 pieces of student art or some combination of the two. The completed "art screening instrument" and accompanying documentation for each child must be submitted by next Friday. New teachers have been told by the veteran Redbud teachers that only 15 students of the 611 enrolled in Redbud Elementary can be admitted to art class.

Week 22, January 29–February 2: Another House Fire

Third and Fourth Grades

A headline of a front-page article in a local newspaper states, "Teachers Get Locked Down but Paid Up: Educators Bust Out of Schools for Better Pay." The article reports, "Glenda Joshua had to go to prison to get her freedom. The former public school teacher was frustrated with low pay and overcrowded classrooms, so she sentenced herself to teaching in the criminal justice system."[1]

The principal of the Swanson Correctional Center for Youth, Ally Williams, notes that he gets inquiries every week from teachers.

"There's no turnover here," Williams said. "When they come here, they never go back to public schools."

All Redbud Elementary teachers receive the following memorandum:

> Teachers,
> Try using the lesson plans given to you at the last faculty meeting for a week.
> Review the two lesson plans and give your grade rep feedback (sections most useful, changes that may need to be made to better fit your grade level, etc.). We will meet with the grade reps next week to discuss the plans.

Third Grade

The third-grade teacher takes her paycheck to the local bank. The teller deposits it and makes the unsolicited remark, "That's not much money for a month's work." She should know. She sees a lot of monthly paychecks.

The children are resourceful. The class finally receives a new pencil sharpener. The electric one that the teacher bought for the class at the beginning of the year is now held together with many strips of masking tape and makes an ominous, high-pitched sound each time it is used. The electrical outlet is distant from the sharpener, and several children have accidently knocked the sharpener to the floor when stepping over the stretched cord. The custodian installs the new manual sharpener on top of an old wooden cabinet.

The first child to use the sharpener tells the class that the handle is on the wrong way. To use the sharpener, the child must crank the handle toward herself with her left hand. Several of the children know the solution to the problem. Jaheesa demonstrates. She squeezes around to the back of the cabinet so she can sharpen her pencil with her right hand moving the handle away from her. Too bad this type of problem solving isn't on the Iowa or state test.

The children need a little brushing up on former presidents and traditional American symbols. When given a group of uncolored pictures for the month of February, Chikae colors Abraham Lincoln black, Antinesha colors a bald eagle green, and Manuel says, "I don't know Jack about this bell, but it looks like somebody dropped it." It is a picture of the Liberty Bell.

Fourth Grade

Earvin isn't in school today. Rachael and Lynette, who live near him, report that his house was on fire yesterday. "The outside is still standing, but the inside got all burned out. Somebody was cooking on the stove," reports Rachael.

The teacher asks if the family is okay. Lynette volunteers, "Earvin's mama had a new baby a month ago, but they are all okay. But everything got all burned up." Redbud teachers will look into getting clothing for Earvin. Rachael and Lynette don't know where Earvin and his family are living. This is the second of the fourth graders in Room H to lose everything in a house fire.

Week 23, February 5–9: "He Don't Want Me to Read"

Third Grade

Something is on Randall's mind. When the class is given a creative writing assignment, he slams down his right hand on his desktop. The teacher calls

Randall to a quiet corner of the classroom where there are two chairs; the other children are working with Ms. Schwartz.

"What's the problem, Randall?" the teacher inquires.

"I can't write anything," Randall says huffily.

"Yes, you can. You've got a good brain," she replies as she points to his head.

"You think somebody who got all Cs and a D on his report card has a good brain?" he asks.

"I know you can improve your grades, Randall. I know the work that you can do when you want to. Is something bothering you?"

"I need a therapist," he confides.

"Why?" the teacher asks.

"Because I can't sleep. I was up until 10:00 last night thinking about my new stepdad. I don't like him and he don't like me."

"Is he hurting you?" she inquires.

"He's not hitting me, but he watches war movies all the time and he makes me watch them. When somebody gets blown up, he laughs and says, 'They got him!' I don't think kids should watch that stuff."

"Can you tell him you'd rather read a book?" the teacher suggests.

"He don't want me to read. But I have a little book hidden under my bed. Sometimes I can read that if it's not too dark."

The talk veers into areas that the teacher promises to keep confidential. He says, "If you tell any of it, I'll get a whipping."

Randall seems to be calmer and goes back to his desk. Later in the day, however, he is staring off into space through teary eyes.

Fourth Grade

Earvin is back in school this week. He says that his family lost almost everything in their house fire. "Now we are living with my aunt," Earvin reports in his soft voice and with his usual shy smile. He may be small in size, but he is big in courage.

Third and Fourth Grades

Redbud police have arrested and charged a 29-year-old man in connection with the murder of the 49-year-old grandmother. He lives one block from the murder scene, which some say is a crackhouse. The accused man has a son at Redbud Elementary School. The police suspect that other people may be involved in the crime.

Third Grade

Wendice smells strongly of cigarette smoke. The children report that they have seen Wendice smoking. The teacher calls him outside the classroom. "Wendice, are you smoking cigarettes?" she asks.

"Yes, ma'am," he replies.

"But you're only 9 years old. Where do you get them?"

"My brother sticks them in my mouth."

"Tell him to stop," she says firmly. "By the way, you aren't working as hard as you should be."

"I know. I'm lazy," he states matter-of-factly.

At the end of the day, Wendice puts a note on the teacher's desk:

> I love you
> I'm very sorry
> What I did
> Bad thing
> Not working

Third and Fourth Grades

Today the school holds two pep rallies. The first is for children in grades 1, 2, and 3, who will take the Iowa Test of Basic Skills next month. The children are brought into the gymnasium and are seated on the floor by grade level. They look so tiny and trusting. The first speaker, the mayor, tells the children that a very important day is coming up. "What day am I talking about?" he asks the children.

"Valentine's Day," a small voice responds. Many little heads nod in agreement. The oldest among them, with the exceptions of those who have been retained, have been on Earth only 9 years.

The second pep rally is for fourth graders. Pam Porter begins by speaking about the state test that the students will take on 5 consecutive days, March 12–16. She stresses the importance of each person's score to himself or herself but also to the school's rating. Next a panel of fifth graders who passed the state test last spring presents their tips:

"Stay calm. If you don't know one, go on to the next one."

"Get lots of rest and eat a good breakfast."

"Study hard every day."

"Listen to the directions."

"Don't be afraid of the test."

The mayor of Redbud is the next speaker. He gives an inspirational speech. He tells the students how much he believes in them and their abilities. The pep rally ends with more words of encouragement from Pam Porter. Everyone leaves the gym in good spirits, having participated in a new phenomenon in American education: pep rallies for high-stakes tests.

Week 24, February 12–16: "ECONOMICS: Interdependence and Decision-Making"

Fourth Grade

Fourth-grade teachers are asked to send home a booklet for each student's parent or guardian. The 24-page booklet contains sample state test mathematics and language/reading questions as well as sample student responses to writing prompts. Before listing 10 test-taking tips, the booklet includes seven pages of questions and answers:

> Q: With such an emphasis on testing, won't teachers "teach to the test" and ignore other topics important to the overall education of students?
> A: It is a fact that tests drive instruction. However, if the tests measure what students should know and be able to do, then it is appropriate that teachers incorporate LEAP 21-type work into their daily teaching.[2]

One might question whether tests measuring such state standards as the following are developmentally appropriate for fourth-grade children:

> Strand E: ECONOMICS: Interdependence and decision-making
> Standard: Students develop an understanding of fundamental economic concepts as they apply to the interdependence and decision-making of individuals, households, businesses, and governments in the United States and the world.

How many adults understand the notions of supply, demand, and scarcity or the causes and effects of inflation and recession? How many American adults know about foreign economic systems? Are adults aware of the fundamental concepts that undergird world economic interdependence? Most of the fourth graders have never been more than 50 miles from home. Where is the developmentally appropriate curriculum that would assist teachers in helping students grasp these economic complexities?

Third Grade

Randall comes up to the teacher's desk. He looks especially disheveled this morning. "My mom and dad were fighting again last night," he tells her. "I was hiding under my bed. One of these days, I know I'm gonna hear a 'pow.'" Randall pulls an imaginary trigger on an imaginary gun.

Third and Fourth Grades

After lunch, all classes are called by grade to the gym. As the students file in, they are greeted by flashing lights and bouncy music. Standing in front with Pam Porter is a stylish gentleman in a coat and tie. The four large tables behind the man are covered with a black tarp, and the image of an order form fills a large projection screen. The children are subjected to a world-class sales pitch to sell "gifts" from a glossy, multicolored catalog.

The catalog items include wind chimes, chocolates, magazines, candles, picture frames, stuffed animals, and more. Prices range from $4.50 to $19.95. The goal is for each student and parent or guardian to sell at least 10 items or more between now and February 26. Doing so, the children are told, will earn the school a lot of money for new computers and software.

Then the pitchman, like a magician, snatches the tarp to reveal the prizes the children can earn for reaching their quotas. The children gasp at the riches displayed on the table. He demonstrates a few: a small, handheld, battery-operated fan that can be used on hot days; a portable radio in the shape of a cell phone; and a lava lamp look-alike with swishing antennae.

He begins his pitch by asking how many children can sell 100 gifts. Every hand goes up. "We're not asking you to sell 100 or even 50 or 30—just 10. Sell only to family and people you know very well. Don't go out at night or knock on strangers' doors. Just sell to your relatives. They don't have to live in Redbud. They can be anywhere in the United States. How many of you can sell 10 gifts by the 26th?"

Every hand goes up. Each class walks out in time to the peppy music as the strobe lights flash. Apparently, poor schools must subject children to this kind of pressure to obtain needed equipment that more affluent schools already have.

Fourth Grade

Yolande is back in school. She lives with her grandmother, who adopted her. Yolande has missed more than 70 consecutive days of school this year. The Families in Need Service has an intervention this morning. Yolande must either return to school or be removed from her home. Yolande is accompanied by her grandmother, who says to the teacher, "I will support you."

In the classroom, the students give Yolande welcoming applause. Despite the efforts by the school and the truant officer, she has been roaming the streets for the past 3 months. This repeats her pattern from last year, when she was a second-year third grader. As the day goes on, it becomes clear that Yolande is considerably behind her classmates in reading and writing skills.

Week 25, February 19–23: "Hire Substitute Teachers"

Third and Fourth Grades

There was no school on Monday because of the Presidents' Day holiday. Tuesday is a professional development day for the district faculty. Professors from a nearby university present sessions throughout the day.

One of the new teachers attends a session called "Teacher Collaborations." There are only two attendees at the presentation, and there are two presenters. The first presenter suggests that the poor attendance makes his point that teachers aren't interested in collaboration and that many don't even know what it is.

The session is a nonstop insult to teachers. The presenters' handout states that some teachers "do not possess sharing skills, protect their autonomy and independence, lack a sense of efficacy, equate avoiding collaborations with avoiding conflict, and view it (i.e., collaboration) as little more than 'window dressing.'" An attendee points out that the teachers she works with want to collaborate but that there is no time during the day. One of the presenters glibly says, "Do it during your lunch hour."

"We must eat with our children and we have only twenty minutes to get their hands washed, get them in line, have them eat, line them up, and march them back to the main building to use the restroom and get to music or phys. ed."

"Well then do it after school."

"Most of the teachers tutor after school, have papers to grade and lesson plans to review, and several have an hour to drive before they get home," is the response.

"Hire substitute teachers," says the increasingly annoyed presenter.

"There's no money to hire subs," replies the attendee.

"Collaborate on Saturdays. I work on Saturdays," the presenter shoots back.

Other remarks from the presenters include, "Teachers are bickering and not listening to one another. Teachers' thinking is conditioned. Men in our study said that the women in their school don't have anything in common with them." The attendees have not found these overgeneralizations to be accurate.

A note in teachers' mailboxes reminds them that the high school cheerleaders will be at Redbud Elementary on March 2 to judge the winning cheer for each grade. These are not cheers for a sports team. These are cheers for the Iowa test and LEAP test. The cheerleaders will select the best cheers from grades 1, 2, and 3 and the three top cheers from grade 4. All these winning cheers will be presented during another pep rally on March 9—the Friday before testing week.

Fourth Grade

Thursday is the last day that Room H's student teacher, Ms. Hammond, is with the class. This African American soon-to-be teacher has been a role model for the children. She is strong, talented, and caring. The class has a little party with refreshments, and each child stands up and says a few words. Ms. Hammond's eyes are not dry for long. Jatoyia sings her rendition of a farewell song that puts a lump in everyone's throat. Each student presents Ms. Hammond with a colorful, homemade good-bye card.

Ms. Hammond will not apply for a position at Redbud Elementary School because the starting salary in Minden, her hometown 20 miles away, is $6,000 higher.

Third Grade

Jelani has his picture in the local newspaper for being rescued from a fire. Teachers bring Wal-Mart plastic bags of clothing and other items to the classroom for Jelani and his siblings. Three children in Rooms B and H have lost everything in home fires this school year: Emerald, Earvin, and now Jelani.

Week 26, February 26–March 2: "A Real Mouse"

Third and Fourth Grades

While driving through a business area during the weekend, the new teachers spot a sign outside a commercial building that reads, "The Reading Center Can Help Students Prepare for the LEAP or Iowa."

"More help for those who have the money," one of them mumbles.

Fourth Grade

Tony tells the teacher that he was in Baton Rouge on Saturday. "Oh, what did you do there?" the teacher asks.

"Went to see my daddy with my grandma. We go a lot."

Tony's father is in Angola, Louisiana's maximum-security prison.

"Will he be there much longer?" the teacher inquires.

"A long time. He might never get out. I look like him."

One of the veteran Redbud Elementary School teachers says that Tony's father is serving a life sentence for murder.

The pending state test is beginning to show its effects on some of the students. Dario, who has not been ill all year, reports every day that he has a bad stomachache. Carlonna says the same thing. Rashand tells the teacher that he is so nervous he doesn't know what to do. Rashand failed the state test last spring and summer and is now in fourth grade for the second time.

The teacher tries to reassure him that he is a bright, capable boy who can easily pass the test this time if he will just relax and stop worrying about it.

Third Grade

Room B is getting closer to having an Internet connection. An unidentified woman appears during class time to examine a computer. She reports, "You got a mouse problem here."

The teacher asks, "What's wrong with the mouse?"

She replies, "Not that mouse. A real mouse. It chewed through your cable. I'll get you a new one."

"Thanks," says the teacher.

NOTES

1. E. O'Brien, "Teachers Get Locked Down but Paid Up: Educators Bust Out of Schools for Better Pay," *News-Star*, January 29, 2001, 1.

2. Louisiana Department of Education, *Reaching for Results: LEAP 21, Grade 4* (Baton Rouge: Louisiana Department of Education, 2001), 7

Chapter Six

"The People in Washington Should See This School"

March, April

Week 27, March 5–9: "I Don't Know the Words"

Fourth Grade

Fourth-grade teachers meet to review logistics for next week's state test. Ms. Larson and Ms. Waverly, the two Redbud veterans among the group, walk the others through the process. Testing will occur from 8:00 to 12:00 every morning or longer if students need more time. The state test is not a timed test.

Teachers are given a 68-page test administration manual for fourth grade and are told that they must sign the oath of security and confidentiality statement, which also must be signed by the school test coordinator and the school principal. The penalty for breach of security is stipulated in the manual, and it involves disciplinary actions in accordance with policies and regulations. The teachers don't have any idea what the disciplinary actions are, but they think that the actions must be severe.

New hires learn that the tests are kept secure at all times from everyone—including the teachers. Even during the administration of the test next week, teachers are not to look at the questions in the student test booklets—out of fear, perhaps, that they will help a student with a question. Teachers are to walk around the room, checking to see if the children are filling in their answer-sheet bubbles properly and sequentially, but they must do this without peeking at any student's test booklet.

The veterans warn that state inspectors could appear in classrooms at any time to see that guidelines are followed to the letter. No inspectors came last year, the teachers are told. The security surrounding the test vaguely reminds the new fourth-grade hire of his training exercises in the U.S. Army many years ago.

Third Grade

The teacher had to sign a sheet acknowledging that she took possession of a 69-page state manual for the Iowa test. The manual contains a test administrator's security agreement, which she has to sign. As with the state test, the security agreement also must be signed by the school test administrator and the principal. The manual contains the same warning about "breach of test security" that is included with the state test.

As the teacher wades through the myriad rules and regulations in the evening, she notes that even an "erasure analysis" policy is in force. Apparently, someone or something will examine the number of erasures and will note which incorrect answers are changed to correct answers.

Ms. Marlow, a third-grade teacher, gives the new teacher the "answer folders" for the children in her classroom. Each contains a bar code and preprinted information. For the students who did not attend Redbud Elementary last year, the teacher must supply Social Security numbers, birth dates, and other information.

Each folder requires that the teacher's first initial and first four letters of her last name be printed under two sections that report the child's present math instructor and science instructor. Then she must fill in these 10 bubbles for each child with her number 2 pencil—200 bubbles just for this section of the answer folder.

On another day, Ms. Marlow brings the new teacher an eight-page district test-security handout:

> In the event the test booklets or answer documents are determined to be missing while in the possession of the school, the school test coordinator shall immediately notify by telephone the District Test Coordinator. The designated school personnel shall investigate the cause of the discrepancy and provide the (state) Department of Education with a report of the investigation within thirty (30) calendar days of the initiation of the investigation. At a minimum, the report shall include the nature of the situation, the time and place of the occurrence, and the names of the persons involved in or witnesses to the occurrence.[1]

With the test materials under lock and key and all the signing for manuals and security oaths, the new hire thinks that it would take a more clever person than she to circumvent these procedures. She thinks back to her earlier years as a classroom teacher when giving a standardized test meant that she could use it as one measure of how her students were doing in comparison to other third graders across the country. It revealed some of her pupils' strengths and weaknesses—but she actually already knew them.

Parents, teachers, and administrators understood that the tests were just one indicator of a child's progress. The message to teachers today is that people in positions of authority in state governments do not trust them. This seems to be another byproduct of the accountability movement.

The third graders are tested on several sections of the Iowa test prep booklet. During the test, Gerard comes up to the teacher's desk and asks, "Can you die of lead poisoning? I poked myself with my pencil."

"That's graphite in your pencil and you won't die," she tells him. "Now finish your test. You're being timed."

After the practice test has been completed, Kanzah comes up to the teacher's desk and asks if he can call home. "I went in my pants during the test," he says.

The results of the practice test are dismal. When the children's answer sheets are returned to them, they see papers filled with red marks. "What happened?" the teacher asks.

"I don't know the words," replies Kelvin.

"I can sound them out," adds Jaheesa, "but I don't know what they mean."

"I can't read the math problems," comments Sam. "I'm good in math but not if there's words."

Third and Fourth Grades

The teachers have worked with their pupils since last August, but they cannot seem to make up for lost experiences and large deficits in linguistic maturation. The language acquisition research of Eve Clark, professor at Stanford University, shows that children, on average, learn about 10 new words a day beginning around age 2. This gives them a speaking/listening vocabulary of 14,000 words by the time they are 6 years old.[2]

According to Carolyn Keelem, an experienced kindergarten teacher at Redbud Elementary, that's far from the case with the children at Redbud. Carolyn says, "They come to school lacking an understanding of even the most basic concepts."

It is well established that preschool children acquire their vocabularies through verbal interactions with adults.[3] Ms. Keelem tells the new hires about Dario, the fourth grader who lives with his mother, grandfather, and two siblings. Before starting school, Dario and his siblings were locked in their trailer every time the adults left home. When he started school, he could barely speak and became panicky when he found himself alone in a room.

Carolyn says that many of the children have television as their primary companion before entering Redbud Elementary School.

Fourth Grade

LEAP test saturation continues across the fourth-grade classes. Oral language activities disappeared from the curriculum weeks ago. Social studies and science get merely a mention these days. Written language and math are the high-stakes test subjects. Any child who fails either of these tests must attend summer school and try again. If they don't pass the summer retake, they stay in grade 4 for another year.

Third Grade

Five sturdy boxes are delivered to the third-grade classroom. Inside the boxes are 20 new children's dictionaries. The pupils cannot believe their good fortune. There are colored pictures and contemporary entry words. What a difference some updated teaching materials will make.

It's Friday afternoon, a few minutes from dismissal. Chikae raises his hand. "Can I bring my rabbit's foot to school to help me on the Iowa test on Monday?"

"Yes, you may," the teacher says.

"No rabbits' feet" is one rule that the teacher did not find in the test manuals.

Week 28: March 12–16: Test Week

Third and Fourth Grades

Severe thunderstorms passed through Redbud last night. Many of the children, while exiting the school buses, tell the teachers that they've been awake since 4:00 a.m. Some say that they are afraid of storms.

Third Grade

After morning housekeeping duties, the school test coordinator brings the teacher the Iowa test booklets. She must sign for them. The teacher passes out the coded answer folders and reads from the script in the administrator's booklet. As the children begin the first timed test, Kelvin vomits in his hands and runs to the bathroom. He does not complete the first section. The teacher must document this. Gerard takes one look at the first section and begins to cry. He picks up his pencil and, between sobs, randomly fills in bubbles on the answer folder.

The teacher cannot comfort or encourage the children. She must read the words printed in boldface in her administrator's manual. Throughout the morning, the teacher notices that even her best reader cannot complete the test sections in the time allotted. When the first day's test sections are finished, the test coordinator collects the stack and answer folders. Again, the teacher must sign her name to indicate that the materials have been collected. Then they are locked up in a location unknown to the teacher.

Fourth Grade

The morning LEAP test consists of two parts. Part 1 asks students to write a descriptive essay of 100 to 150 words. They may use a dictionary and a thesaurus. Part 2 requires that the children use resource materials such as a table of contents, glossary, copyright page, and more. Each test counts for 20% of their total language score.

Before the children entered the classroom this morning, the teacher placed a small pile of books by the desk of each student. This gives them something to read when they finish the test without going to the bookshelf. A few completers riffle through the books. LaDelle, Joshua, and Milo put their heads on their desks and fall asleep.

In the afternoon, the teachers compare notes about how things went. Each teacher mentions that several children finished the resources part of the test in a few minutes. "The child just went down the answer page filling in bubbles" is a recurring comment. Teachers report that numerous students wanted to ask questions about the two "constructed response" questions. Teachers are not allowed to look at the test questions, so they only can surmise that these two questions must be particularly difficult or ambiguously worded. The consensus among fourth-grade teachers is that a number of the pupils just want to get the test behind them.

Third and Fourth Grades

Before school starts, the teachers' attention is briefly diverted from the Iowa and state test administration under way. Immediately after the Pledge of Allegiance, the intercom announces, "Teachers, grade reps will pick up your lesson plan books and grade books now. Thank you." This unannounced inspection of teachers' planning and record keeping, amid all the test pressures, comes as a surprise. "I didn't even do a plan for this week," says Ms. Waverly, "because all we're doing is the LEAP test. My plan book is at home." Once again, teachers are being monitored.

Third Grade

After the teacher turns in her plan book and grade book to the grade-level rep, she notes that Sam has started to cry. "What's wrong, Sam?" she asks.

He sobs, "My dog got hit by a diesel last night and I had to bury him." Other children comfort Sam with tales of pets that have died. This seems to help. Now the teacher must sign for and pass out the test booklets, or she will be behind schedule. Haden falls asleep between test sections. It is difficult to wake him to continue with the testing.

While the children are on a 10-minute recess, the teacher hurries to the staff room to locate a form. Ms. Marlow seems glad to see her. She is standing next to a cumbersome cart. The cart holds several closed boxes. "Will you watch these while I use the bathroom?" she asks.

"Sure," is the reply. "Is there anything good in them?"

"The Iowa test booklets," Ms. Marlow answers. "I'm not supposed to leave them unattended, but I can't get this big cart in the bathroom with me. I tried. There isn't room for me and the cart." The teacher agrees to guard the boxes for the few moments that Ms. Marlow is in the restroom.

Fourth Grade

Perry asks if he can keep the LEAP test booklet when he is finished. "That is forbidden," the teacher responds. "Everything must be turned in to the state." The fourth graders have completed the English language and math sections of the test by Wednesday. Ms. Waverly, the fourth-grade test coordinator, spends hours collating the tests and answer booklets and matching their code numbers with a master list to be certain that everything is accounted for. Each day these test materials must be locked up until they are sent to the state. "Do you get paid extra for this?" the new hire asks her.

"Of course not," she answers. The only people who don't seem to get paid for the extra work are the teachers. The test developers, publishers, vendors, and scoring firms are cleaning up. So are the private test-preparation enterprises for the well-to-do and the writers of test-prep booklets and software sold to the schools.

Third Grade

It is the last day of the Iowa test. As the pupils fill in answer-folder bubbles, a child sneezes. "Bless you," says a chorus of third-grade voices. The voices remind the teacher that in the stark, serious realm of standardized testing where pupils, teachers, and schools will be judged without compassion, she is working with children.

While the teacher was not watching, Antinesha used a pen instead of a number 2 pencil for some answers in a test section. She must report this to the test coordinator. When the teacher does, the coordinator says, "I'll have to call the state to find out what to do."

Antinesha is crying.

"Why did you use a pen instead of the pencils?"

"Because these pencils aren't any good. You can't erase good with them, either."

"You didn't finish a lot of the test. Is something bothering you?" the teacher inquires.

"My grandpa fell and hurt his leg last night and has to have surgery." Antinesha is close to her grandfather. Her father does not live with her, and she never mentions him.

Fourth Grade

After each of the four subject-matter tests on the LEAP, students answer a 15-item multiple-choice questionnaire. For some reason, the manual directs teachers to read these questions aloud—even though they were not allowed to look at the test questions. The teacher surmises that someone wants to make certain these questions are answered by everyone because several of them gather data about the teachers.

Questions ask children how often they use the library for pleasure or research (there is no library at Redbud Elementary), whether they receive comments from their teachers about their writing and suggestions for improving their writing, and how often their teachers explain in writing how their social studies work will be graded.

The LEAP test finally ends at midday on Friday. The children are relieved that it is over. Rashand says, "My brain hurts." Dwayne, De'Lewis, LaDelle, and Nikeya smile for the first time all week.

"Will you grade these this weekend?" inquires Jaylene. Students seem shocked to know that they will have to wait 6 or 8 weeks before learning whether they passed.

Third Grade

The children must complete a questionnaire at the end of the Iowa test. The test administrator's manual states that the teacher can read the questions and choices to the pupils. Some of the questions ask about computers in their homes (most of the pupils have no computer), calculators (there are no calculators in the classroom, and most pupils have none at home), library use (there is no school library), and attitudes toward art (there are no art classes). This is one section of the Iowa that all the children can complete confidently.

The teacher collects the answer folders, math scratch paper (which must be turned in to the test coordinator), and test booklets. She tells the children that they now are finished with the test.

"Thank you, Lord," says Wendice.

Week 29, March 19–23: The Testing Never Ends

Fourth Grade

Yolande, who has been absent nearly 90 days this year, missed 3 of the 5 LEAP test days. This week she has missed the 2 makeup days. The State Department of Education is called about this matter. Their response is that Yolande will get a 0 on the LEAP test, and this 0 will be part of the calculation of Redbud Elementary School's rating. Yolande lives with her grandmother, who has adopted her but seems to have little control over her. The school has reported the situation to social services numerous times.

The students are in a bad mood this week. They argue and fight. After 5 days of LEAP testing last week, this week they face 3 days of Iowa testing. The Iowa testing is mandated by the superintendent, who wants to compare Redbud Elementary fourth graders with those at Hines Elementary, another school in the area.

All this testing has produced increased agitation and anger. Everyone's nerves are frayed, including the fourth-grade teachers'. The hope is that spring break next week will have a calming effect, because the teachers have learned that following the vacation there will be 2 more days of LEAP testing. Its purpose is to "field test" next year's LEAP test.

Third Grade

Several staff members are in a state of near panic, especially Pam Porter, the principal, and Ms. Marlow, the third-grade test coordinator. A third-grade Iowa test booklet is missing during the "official count" of the test materials being readied for the state. This is taken seriously. The rumor is that the state will send someone to Redbud Elementary to give polygraph tests to determine who took the book.

This is yet another manifestation of the paranoia about test security. Why should anyone care if a booklet is missing? The testing is over. What market value could an old Iowa test possibly have? Classrooms are being inspected. Trash in the dumpsters is being opened, and Ms. Marlow, wearing latex gloves, examines it piece by piece. The new hires have never seen anything like this in all their years in education. This is another offshoot of high-stakes testing and the labeling of children and schools.

One of Jimmy's teeth broke off. Leon has a wet paper towel applied to a sore tooth, and Cherise has a bleeding lower gum around a tooth.

During math class, Randall sits so that the soles of his shoes are visible to the teacher. The toe areas on both shoes are worn through. Fragments of dirty white socks can be seen, as well as some bare toes. The teacher doesn't know how long his shoes have lacked bottoms.

Ms. Newburg, a special education teacher, has given Jelani an individualized diagnostic reading test. She tells the third-grade teacher that Jelani has climbed from the kindergarten level at the beginning of the school year to a current second-grade level. This remarkable gain will not show up on the Iowa test. He remains below grade level.

Pam Porter calls the teacher to the principal's office. A man is sitting in a corner of the room. Pam says that he is waiting to collect the Iowa test materials. She also tells the teacher that she has received word about the child who used a pen for some items on the test. The teacher must recopy all the child's answers using a pencil. Pam is too kind to tell her to do this immediately, but the man in the office is hint enough.

The teacher takes the child's test to her room and a blank answer folder. She must have a witness watch her and check her accuracy and honesty— even though she does not have at test booklet. After the dismissal bell rings, the teacher fills in 427 bubbles with a witness at her side.

Third and Fourth Grades

> Survival
> We did it! We survived *the tests*. Even with all the tears and upset stomachs, we survived. Now maybe we can get back to teaching kids.
>
> —Comment from an end-of-the-week Redbud Elementary School newsletter placed in teachers' mailboxes

Week 30, April 2–6: A Bad Label for Redbud Elementary

Third and Fourth Grades

The week begins the day after April Fool's Day, and the children are filled with tricks. Teachers are told that they have spiders crawling on their heads, worms on their legs, and roaches in their ears. As funny as the pupils find these gags, the teachers know that they aren't beyond the realm of possibility.

A faculty meeting is held after school on Monday. The school must participate in a state-mandated self-analysis. A teacher committee is charged with disseminating and tabulating questionnaires and arranging for faculty focus-group discussions. An administrator from the district explains that teachers must do this because Redbud Elementary probably will be designated a "school-improvement school." This is a bad label. It incorporates three levels. In level 1, changes will be required.

The teachers don't yet know what those changes will be, but they might include the reassignment of teachers within the district. In level 2, which is worse, "distinguished educators" will be sent to the school to turn things around. If Redbud is designated a level 3 school, the bottom of the barrel, the state government will make changes, which could include closing down Redbud Elementary. "Where will 611 children go then?" a teacher asks.

"I don't know," the administrator responds. "It could be a veiled threat." The teachers are given a 60-item questionnaire to complete the following day. All teachers must sign for the questionnaire when they receive it, and they must sign again when they turn it in the following day between 2:30 and 3:30 p.m. Although the questionnaire is anonymous, a teacher/monitor has been assigned to a room to receive the questionnaires and signatures.

Some of the items on the questionnaire are ambiguous, and a response would require clarification, but no room is provided for comments. For example, "Students at this school can do better school work than other students." Other students where? Does the item mean that Redbud students could do better if provided the requisite resources for teaching and learning? Does it mean they can do better than students at an even poorer school (if there is one)? At a selective magnet school or laboratory school? Of what use could such opinions be when they are suffused in such ambiguity?

Fourth Grade

Two days of LEAP test "field testing" are mandated now by the state. Students have lost all zest and simply go through the motions of taking these tests of reading, writing, proofreading, and using reference materials. They have been taking standardized tests since March 12. While the children are writing, the teacher thumbs through the administrator's manual. The purpose of this test is to determine the best items to include on the state test for next year.

The new hires have been told by a state legislator that the state will spend more than $56 million each year on its accountability testing program. They can't begin to estimate the additional costs being paid by school districts for expensive electronic and print materials purchased in the hopes that students will get higher test scores. This troubles the teachers in a school that has no hot water for the children, no library, no playground equipment, no art classes, a shortage of textbooks for each child, and uncertified teachers in some of the classrooms.

Third Grade

The teacher reads the book *Follow the Drinking Gourd* to the class. It is a story about how slaves escaped to freedom by looking for the Big Dipper (the Drinking Gourd) pointing toward the North Star. The children are intrigued by the story and are surprised to learn that stars can make a shape. She introduces the word *constellation* to them and goes to the donated encyclopedia set to look for examples. The *constellation* entry is text only.

The class still does not have an Internet connection. She tries to draw a few constellations on the board. The teacher does not want to be resentful, but she thinks of a well-funded laboratory school in a nearby town that can turn children away. Parents must apply to send their children to the school. Some parents put their children on the waiting list when they are born. There is a planetarium adjacent to the school building. This school is labeled a "school of academic achievement" by the state.

Leon falls asleep during math class. Shantel, who sits next to him, suddenly swats his arm.

"What's the matter?" the teacher asks.

"Leon's got a roach on his arm." The teacher gets her flyswatter.

While on recess duty, one of the third graders comes to the teacher and tells her that his mother has left home and that she hates him. Another pupil is standing nearby.

"Don't worry, it's okay," he tells the distraught child. "My daddy hates me. He hasn't seen me or talked to me since I was 6 months old." He puts his arm around the upset child. There is no school counselor at Redbud; the children and their teacher have assumed that role.

Week 31, April 9–12: Dress Code

Third Grade

Leon cannot seem to stay awake today. "What time did you go to bed last night?" the teacher asks.

"I went to sleep at 2:30," he responds.

"That's too late for you. What were you doing until 2:30 in the morning?" she inquires.

Leon, says, "I couldn't sleep because it was too noisy. River Bottom always is noisy when it gets hot outside."

Third and Fourth Grades

Ms. Dawson calls each grade level into the gym to give a lecture to the children about their behavior. The pupils have spring fever. They are becoming increasingly restless. Spats and tattles are on the rise. Ms. Dawson is trying to keep the lid on. As a part of her lecture, she asks several children to stand as she reviews the school's dress code. The children, relieved to be dressed according to the code, are heartbreaking.

The new hires have become inured to the conditions of their pupils' clothing. They don't notice the hand-me-down men's pants that some of the third- and fourth-graders wear. The teachers are so accustomed to seeing holes in shirts, socks, and shoes that such things have become part of the uniform. The teachers' perceptions have changed. It is only when they see the children from a distance—spatially and psychologically—that they notice the state of their clothing. Many are pitiful to look at. The teachers know what is under their students' attire: courage, resilience, and expectations that everything will turn out all right.

The teachers have found that art projects have a soothing effect on the children. Those who want to integrate art into the curriculum must buy the supplies out of their own pockets. There is no budget for materials.

The third- and fourth-grade teachers combine their classes and paint rocks that the children have found in the neighborhood. The medium is tempera paint, and the message is to create any object—real or imaginary—from the rocks. The children are intrigued with the process of applying paint to a variety of surfaces. The room is silent as all concentrate on the project. Their works of art include a piece of pizza, a cave, a whale, a ladybug, a hillside with flowers and a snake, a rat, a racing car, and more. The pupils take great care with the paint and brushes—not a drop of paint is wasted, and the brushes are thoroughly cleaned.

"I made this one for you," Earvin says to his teacher. It is a rock with a red initial on a black background. Even though Earvin just lost everything in a house fire, he is willing to part with something that he made with pride.

Week 32, April 17–20: "The People in Washington Should See This School"

Third Grade

Today the teacher is disgusted with no one in particular but with school-related issues in general. The time off for religious holidays has removed her from the harsh world of Redbud Elementary for a few days. Now it hits her hard. Jelani has been ill all day with a high fever. He has tried to reach someone at home repeatedly, but there has been no answer.

There is no place for Jelani to lie down, and there is no school nurse. She is at Redbud Elementary School on Tuesday mornings only. Ms. Tomah, the second-semester student teacher, dampens a coarse, brown paper towel soaked with cold water and applies the towel to Jelani's forehead. He stays slumped over at his desk all day.

There is a bright spot today. The class finally got an Internet connection—5 weeks before the end of the school year.

Third and Fourth Grades

The third-grade teacher's 80-year-old relatives visit Redbud Elementary this week. The guests, who have not been in public schools in decades, were rattled by what they witnessed. They were upset by the condition of the building and lack of basic instructional materials. "The people in Washington should see this school," commented one.

The guests also were struck by the grueling day that classroom teachers put in. "They're treated like peons. They don't even get a lunch break," the guests noted. These observations were made by two people who lived through the Great Depression and fought and had brothers in World War II. They know about hardships and lack. It takes a lot to jar them. Redbud Elementary did.

Fourth Grade

"When will we hear about the LEAP test results?" Verlin asks every day. It has been a month since they took the tests. This long period of waiting for results is stressful to children and teachers. It is a time of anxiety with the undercurrent of potential failure ever present. The children do not know if they will be going to junior high school or if they will be returning to Redbud Elementary next year to be in class with the present third graders.

Third Grade

Jaron proudly shows the teacher his new pair of shoes. The poorly made shoes are several sizes too big for him. "They make me look taller," says the smiling, diminutive child. All day he trips and stumbles in the ill-fitting shoes.

Manuel reports, "I got my hair cut last night and some guy came into the barber shop and almost fell down. He had one of those big ol' cans of beer with him. I mean a *big* ol' can of beer."

"That's a 40-ouncer," comments Leon.

"My uncle got drunk and hit my aunt and she started smoking again," says Kelvin.

Gerard says, "I saw this TV show once where a man kept drinking and a body part—I don't remember which one—broke. They had to bury him."

Week 33, April 23–27: End-of-the-Year Paperwork

Third and Fourth Grades

The paperwork mounts as the year draws to a close. The first "instrument" for the teachers to complete is a welcome one: the faculty needs assessment form on which teachers list school strengths, weaknesses, school improvement actions, and school improvement barriers. It is the first time that teachers' opinions have been solicited by the state since the new hires began teaching at Redbud Elementary.

A slip of paper accompanying the instrument states, "The needs assessments should be turned in tomorrow in the resource room between 2:30 and 3:30. Each staff member will initial beside their name as they turn in their needs assessment. This will serve as documentation that all needs assessments were completed." This is one form that certainly doesn't need monitoring for completion.

The next instruments that teachers are handed during the day aren't so easily completed. They are the state Department of Education student questionnaires. The questionnaires are to be completed at a specified time on a specified day. Fifty-five minutes of the school day are allotted for student responses. The intention of some of the statements appears to be "checking up" on teachers. For example:

8. I am good in math because of my teachers.
9. My teachers use many different activities to make learning fun and exciting.
23. My teachers use activities that require me to think while using my hands.
27. My teachers keep other students from bothering me while I do my school work.

The students must fill in the appropriate bubbles on the questionnaires with a number 2 pencil if they "strongly disagree," "disagree," "agree," or "strongly agree" with the statements. "Do not know" is another option.

Many of the statements require explanations. In statement 6, for example ("I can achieve in school at or above the level of other students in the nation"), *achieve* must be defined. Statement 7 ("I will attend some form of higher education after graduating from high school, e.g., college, junior college, technical school") necessitates providing definitions for *junior college* and *technical school*. The teachers have to define the word *administrators* in statement 11 ("Administrators help me when I am having problems in my classes").

Some children get lost on the visually complex form and simply fill in bubbles under one option. The classroom teachers must tally all the responses. The third- and fourth-grade teachers each count 740 marks and then send all questionnaires and final counts to the grade reps.

NOTES

1. Louisiana Department of Education, *Louisiana Statewide Norm-Referenced Testing Program: 2001 Test Administration Manual Grade 3: Iowa Tests of Basic Skills Form M* (Itasca, IL: Riverside), 5.

2. Eve Clark, *The Lexicon in Acquisition* (Cambridge, UK: Cambridge University Press, 1993).

3. Jean Aitchison, *Words in the Mind: An Introduction to the Mental Lexicon*, 2nd ed. (Oxford, UK: Blackwell, 1994). Jay Ingram, *Talk, Talk, Talk: An Investigation into the Mystery of Speech* (Toronto, ON: Penguin, 1992). Steven Pinker, *The Language Instinct: How the Mind Creates Language* (New York: HarperPerennial, 1994).

Chapter Seven

The End of a School Year and Recommendations for Policy Change

Week 34, April 30–May 4: "I Don't Want to Spend All My Time on the Paperwork"

Third Grade

The DRA (Developmental Reading Assessment) must be administered to each student again. This is required by the state. Ms. Tomah, the student teacher, works with the class as the regular cooperating classroom teacher individually tests each child. While on playground duty, Ms. Tomah tells the cooperating teacher some disturbing news: She doesn't want to teach in a public school next year. When asked about her decision, she says, "I don't want to spend my time on all the paperwork, and I don't want somebody looking over my shoulder all the time. As a first-year teacher, they'll really watch me."

Ms. Tomah's statements cannot be refuted, but her choice is a big loss for public education. She is one of the best beginning teachers the cooperating teacher has seen. She cares about children, teaches well-planned lessons, and goes the extra mile to see that each child is making progress. If she were to teach at Redbud Elementary, she could help children who others might not reach. If she stayed in public education for 10 years, she could shape at least 200 young lives. Ms. Tomah says that she will take a position, if available, at a private academy rather than deal with state bureaucracy and accountability.

It is Friday. There are just a few moments left before the children leave for the weekend. Ms. Tomah asks the class if they want to sing a song. Two volunteers, Cherise and Antinesha, go to the front of the classroom to lead the singers.

"What would you like to sing?" Ms. Tomah inquires.

"Silent Night," Antinesha replies. All the third graders, sitting in the afternoon sunshine coming in the windows on an 84-degree day, sing "Silent Night."

Week 35, May 7–11: Learning the LEAP Test Results

Third Grade

After lunch, a university supervisor is coming to observe Ms. Tomah's teaching ability. The cooperating teacher tells the children that part of Ms. Tomah's grade will be based on how well she can handle a class, so they should be on their best behavior.

"What if we have to throw up?" inquires Leon seriously.

"Then you may leave without asking," the teacher says. "Now we'd better tidy up this room before she gets here. There's a lot of mud on the floor from the playground."

Jimmy and Kanzah grab brooms. "We can't have it too clean in here, or she'll think something's fishy," Jimmy points out.

Third and Fourth Grades

As a part of a School Improvement Plan, one of the new hires has to complete a form from the state Department of Education titled "Instructional Staff Interview Protocol."[1] It is the basis of a teacher interview conducted by the school improvement team.

Items on the form include: "What new and innovative teaching strategies have you implemented at this school? Explain the staff expectations for you and other teachers at your school. How do your current classroom assessment practices align with assessment strategies in *LEAP/GEE for the 21st Century*? How are curricular issues being addressed in response to the new School Accountability System?" These items are easy to answer. "Teachers teach for the test" answers all four of them.

Another item is, "Explain your role in budgeting fiscal resources (e.g., determining the amount of money spent for Open House refreshments)." This one is really easy to answer. There is no budget for refreshments or for virtually anything else. When asked, "How does your school's policy address children who are excessively absent and/or potential dropouts?" the fourth-grade teacher must answer, "Not well. Yolande has been absent more than 100 school days this year."

Instead of being asked questions such as these, teachers wished that they had been asked, "What can the district or the state do to help you in your teaching? What supplies and materials do you need?"

The new hires run across some figures, given to them by a professor at a local university, that compared last year's LEAP test performance categories and scores. The figures included the percentage of children on free lunch, the percentage of students of color, and the percentage of students in special education.

The comparisons are striking. For example, a school of academic distinction in one district (score 126.6 percent) had 10.9% on free lunch, 8.1% students of color, and 8.8% in special education. A laboratory school rated a school of academic achievement (score 123.5%) had 0% on free lunch, 12.4% students of color, and 3.6% in special education. Last year, Redbud Elementary School, in contrast, a below-average school (score 44.1%), had 88.1% on free lunch (not including those on reduced lunch), 79.1% students of color, and 16.4% in special education.

The teachers look at other schools and see the same pattern—the schools with the highest percentages of students on free lunch, the highest percentages of students of color, and the highest percentages of students in special education achieved the lowest scores on the state test. Even a cursory examination of these statistics for the north-central region of the state shows that no school with a large percentage of free lunch students, special education students, and students of color scored high enough to achieve a label of "above average."

These results stem directly from poverty and its associated ills: lack of medical care, poor nutrition, drug and alcohol abuse, difficulty in finding decent-paying jobs because of little education, and racism.

Third Grade

While on 7:15 a.m. playground duty, Ms. Quigley and the new hire notice a third grader standing alone some distance from the other children and too close to the outside fence. The teachers motion for him to join the others on the playground. "I'm worried about that child," comments Ms. Quigley. "He's essentially homeless. He's moved around from one relative to another. Right now he's living with an aunt. He says his daddy is somewhere in California."

"Where's his mother?" the other teacher asks.

"In the pen for drugs," Ms. Quigley replies.

The pupils make cards for Mother's Day. Some of the children don't live with their mothers, so they make cards for the female adult with whom they live. Wendice is crying. The teacher walks over to his desk. "Why are you crying, Wendice? Are you sick?"

"No, ma'am," he answers.

"Do you need help with your card?" she asks.

"No, ma'am. I don't want to make a card for my mother."

"Why not?"

"Because I don't like her," he sniffs.

"Are you sure? Mother's Day comes only once a year," the teacher reminds him.

"I don't like her and I don't want to make a card for her."

"How about that nice grandma of yours who lives in the country?"

"Okay, I'll make one for her," Wendice says reluctantly.

Gerard tells the teacher at lunch, "When I get out of high school, I'm going straight to the army."

"That can help you pay for college," she remarks.

"Yeah, I want to go to college so I can be one of them lawyers."

"Do you think you'll be rich when you grow up?"

"If I get in that lawyer business I will be. I heard they make $4,000 a year."

"When you're making that kind of money, don't forget about your old third-grade teacher," she says. He smiles.

Fourth Grade

The fourth-grade teachers are summoned to Pam Porter's office at 1:30 p.m. on Friday. Aides are sent to watch their classes. The LEAP results have been released. The teachers learn that 54 of the 118 fourth graders have failed the test and must attend summer school. But these are just numbers. Each number represents a child. If they fail to pass a retake of the exam, they will have to repeat the fourth grade. Fourteen of the 54 children are special education students. The teachers sit stunned as they think about the individuals in their classes who have been with them all year and now have failed. How are they going to tell the children?

Week 36, May 14–18: "They Flunked"

Fourth Grade

Over the weekend, the new hire analyzes the list of students who failed the state test. The teachers have not yet been informed of the performances of those who passed the test. He discovers that six children in his homeroom have failed the English language arts test. Four of the six are in special education, and one is Yolande, who has been truant more than 100 days this year.

Three others, Dario, Tyler, and Derek, failed the math test. Derek's math score was 280, and 282 is a passing score. In his other class, eight children failed the English language arts test—three of whom are special education students. An additional five students failed the math test as well. Andrenna scored 280, and Danielle, who failed both parts of the test the previous year, has scored 279—three points from a pass.

The teacher is filled with anger at the bureaucrats and politicians who designed and mandated this uncompromising accountability system. The Redbud pupils have so many strikes against them. They often are sick. They have rotting teeth and cry because of toothaches. Many come from dysfunctional homes. They are ill-clad and wear ill-fitting shoes. Several do not get enough food or enough rest. They live with acute poverty in substandard homes, often surrounded by drug dealers and users and drunks.

The harsh accountability system imposed by the state kicks them further. The teacher is not opposed to testing. Well-designed tests can give educators useful information. Ideally, the results would inform districts about needs for remediation. Tests should be used to enlighten, not to torment.

Fourth-grade teachers decide that each of them will inform the students of the results in whatever way seems least hurtful. The new hire decides to call his entire class out of the classroom into the hallway, one at a time, in alphabetical order. His first student is Dario. He is told that he has passed the English language arts portion of the test but will have to attend summer school because he failed the math portion. He cries quietly. "My papa [grandfather] gonna be mad at me. He will beat me."

"I'm sure that if you work very hard from June 4 to July 12 you will pass it this summer, Dario," the teacher tells him. "Don't be discouraged. Just be determined to do your best." He reenters the classroom. The teacher's words sound hollow to him. How can Dario not be discouraged? The teacher is discouraged.

The next pupil is Jamal, a special education student. In addition to his speech problems, he has severe learning disabilities. The teacher must inform Jamal that he has failed the English language arts and math portions of the test.

Next comes Jaylene, who has passed both parts of the test and will go on to fifth grade. "Do you mean it? I passed?" She jumps and screams. The teacher tells her to try not to show her joy when she returns to the classroom because children who didn't pass feel bad.

This process continues until the teacher has informed his 12 students who have passed, five of his six students who failed English language arts and math (Yolande is absent), and three others who failed the math portion but passed English. Ms. Avalon, the student teacher, remains in the classroom, reading a story to the class.

When the regular teacher reenters the classroom, most of the children are crying. Those who passed are hugging those who failed and are comforting them. LaDelle tells Chalese, "You'll do fine in summer, Chal." Chalese has severe learning disabilities. She can barely read. This scene is repeated in the hallway and in the four other fourth-grade classrooms.

Third Grade

After school, while the children are sitting in the hallway waiting for their buses to be called, it is nearly silent. The pupils have not been this quiet all year. Sounds of fourth graders crying carry down to where the third graders sit.

"Why are all those kids crying?" asks Jaron.

"They flunked," says Keaziah softly.

The third-grade teacher walks down to the fourth-grade classrooms. She tries to console inconsolable children. The pitiful scene is too much for her. She walks back to her third graders.

Third and Fourth Grades

The new hires are struck by how the decisions of teachers—those who work with the children 176 days (1,232 hours) during a school year—are ignored. Who better to evaluate a student's progress than a certified, experienced teacher who sees all aspects of a child's academic work? Teachers know their students' abilities better than any standardized test score can reveal. They know which children are ready to move to the next grade. Teachers are the experts, but their expertise is brushed aside by the accountability processes.

Some politicians say that the tests are an effort to break the cycle of poverty. This is nonsense to those in the classrooms. Memorizing and cramming for tests do not constitute an education. They help no one. They are not measures of critical comprehension or extrapolation, two qualities of an education that will serve students in their adult years.

There is no art in the Redbud curriculum. Speaking and listening activities have been downplayed because they are not measured on the Iowa or state tests, and science and social studies have taken a backseat to language and math cramming. Some officials and administrators beam with pride because test scores have risen. All this means, however, is that teachers have become better at teaching for the test.

Third Grade

The school nurse comes today. The teacher takes four of her pupils to the nurse. Jelani has been complaining of stomach pains for 2 weeks. The teacher has sent him home, but he returns with the same symptoms. He cries and sleeps most of the time he is in school. Cherise, Kanzah, and Jaron have decayed teeth and bleeding gums. Perhaps a strongly worded letter from the nurse will get the children some help. Leon has nosebleeds, but the teacher already sent him home for the day. She could not stop the bleeding.

In reading class, the children are talking about people overcoming problems. Antinesha tells the class, "My best friend, Alani, has overcome problems. Her real mother went to jail, and her second mother got in a car wreck. But Alani is still okay."

Third and Fourth Grades

Ms. Sauk is angry. One of her second graders has been living in a pop-up trailer in the middle of the woods. The family has no running water or electricity. Ms. Sauk says that the child bathes in a nearby stream and that the family cooks meals over an open fire. She can't get anyone to help the family.

Week 37, May 21–25: Teachers Are an Easy Target

Third and Fourth Grades

Julie Blair reported in *Education Week* that

> lawmakers in Iowa discarded their traditional teacher-compensation system last week and voted to replace it with one that would pay educators based on their performance in the classroom and students' achievement rather than on the number of years spent teaching.[2]

Teachers know that if this practice becomes widespread, educators will run for the wealthy suburbs so that they have a chance of making a living wage. Surely no one would want to teach at Redbud Elementary or in similar schools in the United States where students lack the advantages that elevate test scores. The article quotes Lew W. Finch, superintendent of schools in Cedar Rapids, Iowa, a district with 18,000 students:

> I have yet to talk to a teacher that believes that this new plan will help retain people in the profession. In fact, many of the teachers believe that it will force them to leave the district, and they certainly don't see it as a selling point.

The third- and fourth-grade teachers think that politicians should be held accountable for the condition of schools today. They are the ones who make the laws and control the purse strings. Politicians create the circumstances under which teachers must teach and children must learn. The new hires can think of no other professionals who are held as accountable as educators. Teachers are an easy target, and teacher-bashing is all too common among state and school district officials and policymakers across the nation.

The new hires saw dedicated teachers work small miracles with their pupils every day that they were on the faculty of Redbud Elementary School.

Would it hurt people in power to say, "Teachers, you have done an excellent job bringing these children along as far as you have"?

The Final Week, May 28–June 1: *America the Beautiful*

Fourth Grade

After the morning Pledge of Allegiance, the fourth-grade classes march to the high school auditorium for honors day. The fourth graders are dressed in white shirts and navy blue pants, shorts, or skirts. Jamal said that he didn't own a white top, so the teacher brings Jamal one of his—many sizes too big. With sleeves rolled up several times and the shirt tucked in, he looks fine. Jamal beams when his teacher tells him that the white shirt is a gift. "I'll grow into it," he says without his usual hesitation.

Ms. Quigley has prepared certificates. Today they are awarded to individual children for such achievements as being on the honor roll, having perfect attendance, winning the drug-awareness poster or essay contest, and more. The program concludes with 110 fourth graders who assemble in the front of the auditorium to sing two songs: "Late for the Bus Stop" and "America the Beautiful." More than one parent and teacher brush away tears as they watch these smiling, hope-filled mostly African American children sing in harmony about the wonderfulness of America.

Third Grade

During a discussion of occupations, Manuel states that he wants to be a judge. "My daddy says they make about a million just for sending people to jail." Several hands go up. Many of the pupils tell about relatives who either have been or are in jail. "My stepdad is in jail for selling crack," says one. Another child offers, "My real daddy is in jail for putting a gun to somebody's head." A third child explains that his uncle was involved in an armed robbery.

Third and Fourth Grades

The last few days are spent doing art projects with the children. They make self-portraits using construction paper, yarn, markers, and colored pencils. Pupils make chalk drawings with sidewalk chalk and construction paper. They make butterflies from coffee filters daubed with watercolors. The children are never more quiet or more engaged than when working with art materials.

Thursday is the last day with the children, and time is spent cleaning desks, gathering and stacking books, and just talking. The teachers dispense the last of their stickers, wall hangings, and remaining school supplies. They accompany the children to lunch for the last time at 11:15, where the pupils eat wieners on bread with barbecue sauce, french fries, lettuce salad, and canned pear halves. All teachers stand with their classes as they await the buses and exchange best wishes, hugs, humor, and not a few tears. And then they are gone.

SUMMARY OF RECOMMENDATIONS

First, the use of high-stakes tests in some subjects is changing what goes on in classrooms to the detriment of the arts, problem-solving, creativity, and the joy associated with learning and discovering. In recent years, schools such as Redbud Elementary have become little more than test-preparation centers whose teachers must spend disproportionate amounts of time teaching children how to take tests. Time is spent cramming the materials covered in the tests to the neglect of entire subjects such as science, social studies, art, drama, and music.

Present policies place unwarranted stress on children and teachers because of the intense pressure to raise scores. State legislatures, boards of education, and school district authorities must back off from their commitment to raise test scores at the expense of providing children a well-rounded, well-grounded education across the curriculum. Passing a high-stakes test does not mean that students are well educated any more than passing a written or behind-the-wheel driver's test means that someone is a good driver.

The continual drill-and-practice for the tests leaves the slower learners even farther behind. They become discouraged and give up on school at an early age. There are not enough adults available to help them catch up. States should redirect the money spent on testing into hiring an additional adult for each classroom in underfunded schools. This would be an example of real education reform.

Second, states and school districts must stop making important decisions about grade promotion or graduation based on a single test—even if given repeatedly. Listen to the experts in the classrooms and the professional organizations. Use multiple indicators such as test data, course grades, portfolios, and teacher judgments to determine who passes and who fails. Teachers know their students better than any single test can. They know the strengths and weaknesses and capabilities of the students with whom they work daily, week in and week out.

Third, states that give high-stakes tests should not only reexamine their testing policies but also examine the tests themselves. Who wrote the tests? What are their qualifications? What teaching experience have they had with students of the ages being tested? Who determines the pass-fail scores? On what basis? What are the content validity and reliability of the tests? How developmentally appropriate are the content and format of the tests?

Fourth, schools in American are unequally funded. If every child in a state is expected to take the same test, every school should have the same proportionate quantity and quality of certified teachers; the same quantity and quality of instructional materials and resources; the same school environment in terms of building repair, cleanliness, and absence of vermin; the same playground and recreational equipment; and the same support personnel such as counselors and school nurses.

Children of poverty have so many strikes against them in their homes, neighborhoods, and daily lives that they must, at the least, have the same in-school advantages as children of the middle classes and the affluent if they are to be held to the same standards as measured by the same standardized tests. This means that states must rethink their policies and procedures for funding local schools and must make a financial and moral commitment to equalize such funding.

Fifth, children of poverty must be provided with nursery school and preschool education similar to what is typically available to more economically fortunate children. Many children in schools such as Redbud enter kindergarten and first grade seriously deficient in concept formation, vocabulary, and general language development. There is evidence that preschool programs help young children achieve a more equal footing. State legislation is needed, and the inherent financial commitment must follow, to provide preschool education for all.

Sixth, unequal funding of schools has been an indirect cause of some of the obvious resegregation of schools. The growth of private schools and academies, which often have mostly White students, is a result of parents' unwillingness to send their children to underfunded local schools whose student bodies have become mostly students of color. If this type of resegregation is to be stopped, state and local (and perhaps federal) governments must see to it that public schools have adequate and equal funding.

One might wonder if there isn't an unspoken and unwritten message to the children who attend schools such as Redbud. The message is, "You're Black and poor. A few of you are White and poor. These schools are good enough for you." The message is racist and smacks of social class elitism. State school officials must address this issue. Perhaps it is time for a federal review of these separate and unequal schools.

Seventh, decision-making must again be entrusted to teachers rather than to state and district officials far removed from the classroom. Restore teacher dignity and autonomy by allowing teachers the freedom to teach—to plan and develop engaging and innovative instructional activities. State and district administrators must reduce and preferably eliminate cumbersome burdens of redundant paperwork that currently engulf much of a teacher's time.

They must stop the persistent and unnecessary monitoring of teacher activities and trust them to do their jobs.

Administrators must make life easier for teachers by providing them with time each day away from their children—even if it's just 15 minutes to regroup or use the restroom. Give teachers a lunch period free from lunchroom duties and interacting with pupils.

Eighth, it is time for a national commitment to raise teachers' salaries to a professional level so that they can afford to stay in the profession. No school should have to hire uncertified teachers who are there to mark time and collect a little money before they move on to their careers of choice. Schools must have nurturing, sincere people behind the teachers' desks. Pay raises are especially needed for teachers willing to work in challenging rural and urban schools.

Ninth, underfunded schools need volunteers. It is one thing to talk about social injustice but quite another to do something about it. Parents and guardians who are among the working poor are too weary dealing with the grind of poverty to volunteer their time in schools the way some parents can. Teachers are too beaten down and worn out by the demands of accountability, benchmarks, codes, and other imposed minutiae to give more of themselves. There just isn't enough time or energy.

Volunteers are needed to tutor children and read to them, to staff the lunchrooms so that teachers get a short break, and to paint and decorate classrooms and hallways. Volunteers are needed from organizations and service clubs such as Junior League, Kiwanis, and Rotary.

Volunteers are needed from colleges and universities whose professors in many disciplines could require service projects in poor schools. English and sociology classes could compile guides to food banks, dental clinics, and social service agencies. Business classes could organize and conduct fundraising drives to support local schools. Journalism students could write articles that appeal for volunteers to work in the schools.

As a country, we need to realize what a mistake it is to not nourish, in every sense of the word, children of poverty. The Redbud children showed courage, ingenuity, eagerness to learn, trust, compassion for others, a warm sense of humor, and genuine kindness. Dwight D. Eisenhower, in a commencement address at Gettysburg College in 1946, captured the spirit seen daily in the children of Redbud: "Fortunately for us and our world, youth is not easily discouraged. . . . The hopes of the world rest on the flexibility, vigor, capacity for new thought, the fresh outlook of the young."[3]

Three years after the year the new hires taught in Redbud, results of the Iowa Test of Basic Skills scores still were below the national median of the 50th percentile. The state test scores continued to be below most other districts in the state. What good did all the pressures on the children and all the money spent on accountability do?

Four years after the new hires' school year at Redbud Elementary, the superintendent left for another superintendency in the state, the principal accepted a principalship in another state, the assistant principal left the school, and several teachers with whom they worked moved to other schools or retired. The average salary at Redbud remained among the lowest in the state.

Teachers in Redbud Elementary School now must use a "scripted program" instead of "balanced reading" to teach children to read. The district employs "coordinators" to monitor this "teacher-proof" instruction. Schools currently receive checks from the state Department of Education when they have reached their "growth targets." Those schools, however, that show "growth," but do not reach the targeted number of points set by the department, receive nothing but bad publicity.

The town looks as it did when the new hires taught there. They occasionally saw some of their former pupils' names on the junior high school honor roll—but not enough of them. Poverty and continued pressures of high-stakes testing exacted a toll on young minds and bodies.

In "Standards for What?" Robert B. Reich, former U.S. secretary of labor, pointed out:

> The latest rage in education is standardized tests. Tests have been around for a long time, of course, but have never been employed to the extent they are now. Young people are now being tested and then retested a year or two later, and then retested again and again. Our schools are morphing into test-taking factories. Politicians like tests because they don't cost much money and they reassure the public that children are at least learning something.
>
> Paradoxically, we're embracing standardized tests just when the new economy is eliminating standardized jobs. If there's one certainty about what today's schoolchildren will be doing a decade or two from now, it's that they won't all be doing the same things, and they certainly won't be drawing on the same body of knowledge.[4]

Reich's observations reiterate a warning sounded by former President Harry Truman in 1956:

> People must have freedom of mind for research that makes progress, otherwise there is no use in having an education system. If everyone remained in the same groove and were taught exactly the same thing, we would end up with a nation of mediocrities.[5]

One might fear that the accountability movement that has swept throughout American education, and the high-stakes testing that it spawned, are driving the nation in the direction that Truman warned against.

NOTES

1. Louisiana Department of Education, *School Analysis Model (SAM)* (Baton Rouge: Louisiana Department of Education, 2005). www.doe.state.la.us/lde/ssaa/1591.html.

2. Julie Blair, "Iowa Approves Performance Pay for Its Teachers," *Education Week*, May 16, 2001, 24–25.

3. Gorton Carruth and Eugene Ehrlich, *American Quotations* (New York: Wings, 1988), 633.

4. Robert B. Reich, "Standards for What?" *Education Week*, June 20, 2001, 64.

5. Alex Ayres, ed., *The Wit and Wisdom of Harry S Truman* (New York: Meridian, 1998), 42.

Chapter Eight

The Changing Roles of Teachers

HISTORICAL NOTES ON TEACHERS' LOTS

Tales about education in America offer insights on how schools and those who teach in them have been treated throughout the years. Many early urban schools, for example, were packed to the rafters, sometimes with over 60 students in a single classroom. Some large city schools were located over sewer systems that were visited by wandering pigs in search of snacks.

In one New York City school in the late 1800s, furniture was in short supply, so the students had to "study on their knees." The school was located over a market that sold live chickens.[1] "Teaching in America has always been poorly paid and poorly regarded," wrote Katz.[2] Additional snippets from the 17th, 18th, and 19th centuries have supported Katz's words.

COLONIAL YEARS, THE COMMON SCHOOL, NORMAL SCHOOLS

Teachers during the colonial years usually were men. Many had additional sources of income such as farming, and they used teaching as an interim job until they landed work in a more highly respected career such as law.[3] The Common School movement, circa 1820–1830, guided by Horace Mann (1796–1859), supported free, public, tax-supported education for all. Common schools were noble in intention, but the differences in tax bases affected the quality of learners' experiences in these schools—an issue that still exists today. Also, "for all" usually left out children of color.

To staff the large number of Common Schools, localities turned to women for whom other professions were not easily accessible due to chauvinistic notions. Women often were paid less than men for the same teaching jobs.

Clara Barton, founder of the American Red Cross and noted for her nursing skills on Civil War battlefields, began her adult life as a teacher in a room of 40 students of various ages. In a Massachusetts school district, Barton demanded and received the same pay as her male colleagues; however, this was not the case in other districts where she was employed. After putting considerable effort into a school, she lost the superintendent's position to a man, and that was enough to spur her on to other ways of making a living.[4]

Normal schools (from the Latin *norma* meaning *model*) were established to provide formal training in content and teaching methods to prospective teachers. During the mid- to late 1800s, some teachers had little more education than the students whom they were teaching. Although normal schools offered only two years of education, they were a step toward the professionalization of teaching.

Many universities, from east to west, began as normal schools. The present-day University of Northern Iowa began as an orphanage for children who lost fathers in the Civil War and whose widowed mothers had no way to provide for them. The orphanage became a state normal school in 1876 when the orphanage's services were no longer needed.[5]

The University of California, Los Angeles, began as the State Normal School in 1880. At the time, the population of Los Angeles was 11,000, and aspiring teachers needed to be trained. In 1919, the State Normal School was renamed the Southern Branch of the University of California.[6] Normal schools eventually were subsumed into 4-year universities and colleges, which surely must have increased their academic stature.

Although more education for preservice teachers was expected during the normal school years and those years following, teachers continued to be underpaid. In the 1879, the *New York Times* reported that "teachers subsist on a pittance; they must pinch and save until life is not worth living."[7]

As large numbers of people moved west in the early 1800s, schoolhouses were built by community members. Some schools were made of sod with holes punched through the walls for windows. The one-room "buildings" had dirt floors with desks and benches made by locals; instructional materials consisted of books that parents could contribute. Students of various ages, ranging from 5 to the early 20s, often sat in the same class.

There were no established tax-collection structures in these locales, so teachers were paid according to what parents could afford, and amounts usually were small. Dick wrote, "The West tried to entice teachers trained in the eastern colleges or academies for this work. This was hard to do on account of the low wages offered."[8]

There are reports of teachers going without any pay due to parents' unexpected expenses or unscrupulous community members. Many teachers lived with the families of their students; they rotated from one home to another during the school months for free room and board. Some arrangements were more inviting than others. The author Laura Ingalls Wilder, after receiving her credential to teach, boarded with folks who had a "depressed knife-wielding" family member among them.[9]

Curriculum during these early years was mostly relegated to reading, writing, and basic arithmetic; memorization and recitation were evidence of learning the content. With the large numbers of students in a single classroom, there was no hope for individualized attention. Maintaining order was challenging under such conditions. Bettmann reported, "The Little Red Schoolhouse was not a stable of docile lambs; many of the children were downright brats—hostile, ungovernable and prone to violence."[10]

Dick noted that in one school, "Five or six of the boys from eighteen to twenty years old, weighing 160 to 175 pounds ganged up on the teachers and whipped them as fast as they arrived."[11] Dick also pointed out that it was not always beefy male teachers who could handle such young scholars—it might be females or slight-appearing males who could subdue them.

RETHINKING EDUCATION: THE LIGHT OF JOHN DEWEY

John Dewey (1859–1952), whose academic background was philosophy, is known for his support of democratic principles in what teachers do and what students learn. One can see his influence in wealthy schools today where standardized testing has not become the curriculum.[12]

Dewey invested more of his time at the University of Chicago in education as he watched the development of his own children. He established the Laboratory School in 1896, while at Chicago, where group activities and learning by doing were major components of the school day. Students were encouraged to follow their interests and ask questions, and teachers were viewed as knowledgeable guides during learning episodes.

Carpentry, weaving, and other activities comprised the curriculum. Dewey included cooking as content. Menand wrote that when children were making a weekly lunch, several disciplines were addressed in the completion of the task: "arithmetic (weighing and measuring ingredients, with instruments the children made themselves), chemistry and physics (observing the process of combustion) . . . geography (exploring the natural environments of the plants and animals)," and more.[13]

A particularly valuable principle of Dewey's progressive education pedagogy is its emphasis on transferability of knowledge to present and future life situations. This useful principle is a far cry from the memorization and recitation of discrete bits of information that was prominent in earlier classrooms and a part of the skill-and-drill for testing that is found in schools today.

Chapter 8

POST-DEWEY TO 1983: A GOLDEN AGE FOR TEACHERS

The Soviet Union's launch of the satellite *Sputnik* in 1957 convinced U.S. lawmakers that more federal money should be invested in education to keep America's competitive edge in global affairs. Rather than blame and degrade American teachers during the Soviet's space leap, the U.S. president during this time, Dwight D. Eisenhower, stated, "Teachers need our active support and encouragement. They are doing one of the most necessary and exacting jobs in the land. They are developing our most precious national resource: our children, our future citizens."[14]

The National Defense Education Act, passed in 1958, designated dollars for education research and assistance to teachers through additional training and classroom supplies. Loans with attractive conditions for repayment were made available to prospective teachers.[15] It was recognized that preservice and in-service educators needed financial support for their endeavors.

The years prior to *A Nation at Risk,* published in 1983, were productive learning times (replete with transferable skills) for most students. Educators in many districts were given credit for their knowledge of child development, societal factors that affect learning, and age appropriate content and delivery methods. The following recollection from a third-grade teacher illustrated the freedom under which teachers taught and students learned.[16]

On an unannounced visit, the teacher was introduced to a cohort of scholars from Japan who were visiting classrooms near the University of Wisconsin–Madison, the scholars' host. The teacher's principal explained that the scholars were investigating factors that contributed to American creativity. An examination of elementary school classrooms seemed like a reasonable starting point.

At the time of the visit, the third-grade pupils were making puppets. The children recently had seen a puppet show during an assembly in the school gym, and they wanted to make their own puppets and produce their own puppet show. The teacher had distributed scraps of construction paper and cloth, craft sticks, wire, string, lengths of yarn, and other surplus odd-and-ends on children's desks that had been pushed together. The third graders were told that they could work alone, in pairs, or in small groups.

The visitors were somewhat surprised, it seemed. Where were the directions? Where were the plans? There were none—at least not written down. The teacher knew the skills that would be introduced and honed as the children worked. Pupils had to determine their puppets' character traits and how they would accomplish movement of the puppets' heads and limbs while maintaining balance. They had to consider aesthetic appearances, had to establish a story structure, had to write dialogue (with correct use of quotation marks), had to determine what would serve as a stage, and other tasks related to a well-produced and delivered puppet show.

When asked why there was no formal plan for the puppet show, the teacher said, "Why would I do that? Then the children wouldn't learn anything. They already know how to follow directions." Creativity, problem solving, incorporating writing skills, practicing social skills—the list is lengthy for this type of activity—and each child was engaged. This was not some free-for-all to give the teacher a rest. She was available as a guide to make suggestions—but not to do the job for the pupils.

In preparation for the children's puppet show, no standards were listed on paper or electronically, no future standardized test questions were addressed. One could only imagine what would happen to such a teacher in many schools today—especially low-income schools where test scores are low. The teacher most likely would be reprimanded at best.

1983 TO THE PRESENT: TEACHERS AS SCAPEGOATS

In 1983 during the presidency of Ronald Reagan, the National Commission on Excellence in Education was formed by the secretary of education, Terrel H. Bell. Among the 18 members of the commission were university presidents, businesspeople, a former governor, two principals and a superintendent, two professors, and school board and state-affiliated education personnel. There was one practicing teacher on the commission.[17]

The commission's report, *A Nation at Risk*, stated that America's "educational foundations" were "being eroded by a rising tide of mediocrity that threatens our very future as a Nation and a people."[18] The report, which took 18 months to complete, pointed to Japanese auto manufacturing, the efficiency of South Korean steel mills, and the replacement of American machine tools with German tools as examples of how our economic competitors were minimizing the country's competitive edge. The report's bleak words were addressed to "the American people" rather than to a governmental agency.

The commission recommended five areas that needed attention: content, standards and expectations, time, teaching, and leadership and fiscal support. The areas of standards and teaching proved to be the beginning of the end of the professional autonomy that educators had experienced prior to the report.

Like the Sooners of the Oklahoma Land Rush and the '49ers of the California Gold Rush in the 1800s, at the release of *A Nation at Risk*, publishing houses and some wily academics pounced. There were territories to grab and money to be made. One might excuse educational publishers because they are businesses that must be concerned about the bottom line. One might not be so quick to excuse professors who should be familiar with social science research protocols.

An example from Johnson and colleagues[19] illustrated how having standards for a subject—with which few people would disagree—mushroomed into an unwieldy proposition. If a teacher wanted to teach idiomatic expressions, such as *in a pickle* and *to smell a rat*, the following standards codes would apply: N 1a (this is a code from the National Council for Accreditation of Teacher Education[20]), I 6.1 (from the Interstate New Teacher Assessment and Support Consortium), IRA 1.4 (the International Reading Association[21]), NYS 2.3 (New York State Learning Standards for English Language Arts).

There are more, but these letters and numerals suffice in showing what a foolish burden this could place on classroom teachers who already are astute enough to know that idioms are prevalent in written and spoken English and that they are difficult for those whose first language is not English. Teachers in some districts have been made to put such codes on their lesson plans and in front of the classroom for each lesson taught.[22]

The overemphasis on standards (with the accompanying nitpicking, time-wasting keying and coding) flies in the face of what the National Commission on Excellence in Education warned against: using "beleaguered teachers" as scapegoats when addressing education's shortcomings.

There are questions that should be asked, by curriculum specialists, administrators, and teachers (if they are free to speak without district repercussions) when standards are presented to educators. Who are the people who wrote the standards? When was the last time that they taught in the grades for which they wrote the standards? In what type of school did they teach—well funded or underserved?

Standards usually are drawn up by committees or task forces that have been given that charge by some organization, such as the International Literacy Association (formerly the International Reading Association), or a government body. Committee or task-force members engage in give-and-take discussions about what should be included in the standards. The result often means that a set of standards is a compromise document that accommodates various points of view.

Those who write standards must have considerable blocks of time available for the endeavor. That leaves out most classroom teachers unless they work in a district that has dollars for substitutes during the school year. The monumental task of designing age-appropriate, attainable standards cannot be squeezed into a few summer months.

Although it is not pleasant to think about, there is the possibility that aspects of some standards might be politically motivated or included because of dreams of future profits. A standards writer, for example, whose expertise is in an element of literacy, might be motivated to include such an element not on the basis of teachers' knowledge and experience with an age group, but on prospective sales of the writer's soon-to-be books and supplementary materials that include the element for which the writer is known.

The commission recognized that school improvement requires money. Members wrote, "Excellence costs. But in the long run mediocrity costs far more."[23] If funding for schools had been pursued as avidly as standards development and enforcement, education would look different these days. Standardized testing at certain points of students' schooling was mentioned in *A Nation at Risk*, but it took another federal endeavor, *No Child Left Behind* (NCLB), to markedly alter what transpires in many contemporary classrooms.

NO CHILD LEFT BEHIND

The No Child Left Behind bill (Public Law 107-110) was signed on January 8, 2002. The bill was a portion of the reauthorization of the Elementary and Secondary Education Act of 1965 (signed by President Lyndon B. Johnson as a part of his War on Poverty). There were other federal acts prior to this legislation (e.g., America 2000, Goals 2000), but NCLB so far takes the prize in the federal government's influence in what transpires in public schools.

Under the law, students were to be tested in grades 3 through 8 in reading and math; those schools that did not meet "adequate yearly progress," after set periods of time, ran the risk of being taken over by the state or even closed. Standardized testing flourished, and teaching to the test became common practice. Public shaming of schools, which was initiated earlier with state tests (such as the LEAP test noted in previous chapters), ramped up and continues with ratings in the form of stars, letter grades, and descriptors (e.g., "school of academic distinction," "low-performing school").

No Child Left Behind is a sentiment with which few would argue. What the testing mandates in the law did, however, was leave low-income children even further behind and discourage some competent teachers from remaining in the profession.

Johnson and Johnson pointed out that the "relationship between socioeconomic status and test performance is well established."[24] As the authors noted, this relationship has nothing to do with intelligence and everything to do with opportunities. A bill such as No Child Left Behind would have done more to improve education if it had funded nutritious meals for children on weekends, repaired their leaking and mold-infested classrooms, supplied dollars for up-to-date teaching materials and technology, provided money for field trips, and paid teachers in underfunded schools what their counterparts in wealthier districts received.

Chapter 8

THE COMMON CORE STATE STANDARDS

The Common Core State Standards (CCSS) were introduced in 2009 through the Council of Chief State School Officers and the National Governors Association Center for Best Practices. The CCSS were developed to provide some uniformity among states who had been using their own standards and measurement tools (usually in the form of summative tests).

The flurry to peddle anything related to the CCSS has been impressive. The term *research-based* has become popular; however, the use of the term should require the materials' authors to provide information on basic questions such as: What was the sample size of the research cited? Was it a sample of convenience (i.e., a lab school, for example, near a university that enrolls numerous professors' children)? Who are the investigators in these research-based studies—those with numerous years of teaching experience with the population?

Johnson referred to those who seek profit from whatever topic is in vogue as "peddlers at podia" and "circuit riders."[25] Such profiteers rarely divulge how long ago they taught or in what type of schools. Some peddlers, Johnson noted, are cagey in their presentations—they take a fence-sitting approach to the topic—addressing the good and the sort-of-not-so-good aspects of a topic. This stance, Johnson said, is taken to "not ruffle moneyed feathers."[26] Discussing poor children and their teachers, when addressing a captive audience, would be such a downer.

With the adoption of the CCSS by many states, teachers again bore the brunt of adjusting to new demands. Those educators working in underfunded schools could assume that yet another set of standards, without additional personnel or funds to achieve these standards, would bring the standards' tag-along pal, high-stakes testing, and more bad publicity.

Since *A Nation at Risk*'s recommendation that "schools, colleges, and universities adopt more rigorous and measurable standards,"[27] the education community has seen mountains of standards. As Johnson wrote, however,

> No words on paper or those delivered electronically, without human and monetary support, will improve the education of anyone. . . . Where are the data that all of the time and money spent on the development and implementation of any set of standards . . . have had positive impacts on student learning—regardless of how student learning is measured?[28]

The irony of adopting standards, without financial backing for underfunded schools, is that the standards can exacerbate disparities among socioeconomic groups. Apple wrote:

> [Many] people almost automatically think that having standards (decided by whom?) and testing them rigorously will lead to higher achievement, especial-

ly among our most disadvantaged children. By in essence holding schools', teachers' and teacher education institutions' feet to the fire, so to speak, there will be steady improvement in achievement. Yet, the empirical evidence for this assertion is weak at best. Indeed, a considerable amount of international literature should make us very cautious about assuming that this will be the case. Such policies have been shown to just as often stratify even more powerfully by class and race, no matter what the rhetorical artifice used to justify them.[29]

Although there are other examples, the Common Core's English Language Arts Standards, Vocabulary Acquisition and Use, CCSS.ELA-Literacy.L.1.5 and CCSS.ELA-Literacy.L.2.5, illustrate how age-inappropriate elements favor children who hear words at home that are used in instructional materials, children's literature, and tests.

CCSS.ELA-Literacy.L.1.5 (Grade 1), "With guidance and support from adults, demonstrate understanding of word relationships and nuances in word meanings": "CCSS.ELA-Literacy.L.1.5d Distinguish shades of meaning among verbs differing in manner (e.g., *look, peek, glance, stare, glare, scowl*) and adjectives differing in intensity (e.g., large, gigantic) by defining or choosing them or by acting out the meanings."

What is the difference between *stare* and *glare*? How would a 6-year-old "act out" such nuances? How would most adults fare on such a task?

CCSS.ELA-Literacy.L.2.5 (Grade 2), "Demonstrate understanding of word relationships and nuances in word meanings": "CCSS.ELA-Literacy.L.2.5b Distinguish shades of meaning among closely related verbs (e.g., *toss, throw, hurl*) and closely related adjectives (e.g., *thin, slender, skinny, scrawny*)."

Seven-year-olds are expected to distinguish shades of meaning among closely related words—words such as *skinny* and *scrawny*. That expectation requires a degree of sophistication with English. Although teaching shades of meaning is an important aspect of reading and writing achievement, it is a complex endeavor that requires repetition of targeted synonyms which would, on tests of the standard, give an advantage to children who hear the synonyms used at home as well as in school.

Hall, in a 2014 article, referred to a member of the CCSS validation committee who suggested that teachers should read, in-depth, the standards from beginning to end.[30] That's not too much to ask; teachers have had no choice but to do so, and if their performances are judged on teaching the standards, it would be foolhardy to not read them in-depth.

Pearson, the member whom Hall referred to in her article, stated, "I think people want a little breathing room, a little flexibility, a little prerogative in implementation. If they're savvy about it, [educators] can find that in the standards themselves."[31]

According to Hall, Pearson also stated that the CCSS are "offering educators broad performance goals for students . . . not dictating curriculum."[32] It's easy to speak of the savviness of those who will hunt down the standards' presumptive inherent flexibility, but it's another thing, regardless of a teacher's savvy quotient, to implement a standard, such as the above examples, to a class of 20–30 wiggling first or second graders.

A year prior to Pearson's statements, an article in the *Washington Post* described a veteran teacher who, despite her documented value as an educator, faced a new instructional paradigm with the adoption of the Common Core State Standards. She reported:

> I was given a curriculum and told by my administration to teach it "word-for-word." In a meeting with my administration, I was reprimanded with "Don't forget, standards drive our instruction."
>
> Standards drive instruction. Data determines effectiveness. Positive outcomes for students requires proof.
>
> If I don't supply that proof, I'm not an effective teacher. Period. And my administration has warned me that my job depends on this proof.[33]

That same year, a fourth-grade teacher wrote:

> I was allowed [in years past] to use my professional judgment as a teacher. Since then everything we teach is directed from the top down, and all materials and teachers' editions are scripted. I go to school, put in my time, and then work at least two hours at home each night because planning time is directed by powers that be for math data, literacy data, and lesson plans. In prior years, we taught social studies and science daily. Now we teach 30 minutes of social studies or science four days each week. There's no time for projects or experiments as the district wants us to READ about social studies or science.[34]

Literacy Comprehension 101 teaches that unless readers know the words, the readers cannot completely comprehend the text. For example, in the sentence "*Demy, elephant,* and *crown* were identified," the reader would have to know, for adequate comprehension, that *demy* is a 17.5 × 22.5 sheet of paper, *elephant* is a sheet measuring 20 × 27 inches, and *crown* measures 15 × 20 inches. Office personnel who order paper, and printers and artists who use various paper sizes, probably could comprehend the sentence; those without this prior knowledge would have difficulty.[35]

Johnson and colleauges interviewed economically privileged middle-school students and students from low-income families. They found that no students from affluent families could define food stamps (e.g., "Aren't they the little stickers they put on apples and bananas?"), but all of the low-income students could define the term. All of the students from high socioeconomic status (SES) families could define *orthodontist, passport,* and *board-*

ing pass; none of the low-SES students could define the words.³⁶ As Wexler pointed out:

> The Common Core literacy standards, which since 2010 have influenced classroom practice in most states, have in many ways made a bad situation worse. In an effort to expand children's knowledge, the standards call for elementary-school teachers to expose all students to more complex writing and more nonfiction. This may seem like a step in the right direction, but nonfiction generally assumes even more background knowledge and vocabulary than fiction does.³⁷

Duckworth, in a Harvard Graduate School of Education publication, which also was available in the fall of 2014, pointed out that because so few teachers helped in the development of the CCSS, "I don't have a lot of faith in the standards they would come up with."³⁸ New standardized tests appeared that are tied to the CCSS. As Buttimer wrote, "Standards in the United States have not been and will not be decoupled from testing, nor from the profit motive that's at least partly driving the creation of standards-based reform and test-based accountability."³⁹

When teachers' performances are based, in part, on standardized test scores, and those tests are based on the Common Core State Standards without additional assistance for the teacher, then, as Buttimer stated, "We've skipped right to the evaluate-and-punish stage."⁴⁰ The CCSS might not directly be "dictating curriculum" as Pearson noted, but what would one call it when test scores, teacher evaluations, and a school's public reputation are determined by standardized measurements of the CCSS?

Souto-Manning referred to today's teachers as "technicians" who are given standardized curricula rather than working as professionals who are given opportunities for innovation in their classrooms. She wrote, "After their work is devalued to a deadening uniformity, teachers are then evaluated based on students' test scores."⁴¹

RACE TO THE TOP

The rollout of the CCSS was followed, in 2012, by Race to the Top, which funded states through competitive grants based on the following criteria:

1. "Adopting standards and assessments that prepare students to succeed in college and the workplace and to compete in the global economy";
2. "Building data systems that measure student growth and success, and inform teachers and principals about how they can improve instruction";

3. "Recruiting, developing, rewarding, and retaining effective teachers and principals, especially where they are needed most"; and
4. "Turning around our lowest-achieving schools."[42]

The Race to the Top program description added, "Awards in Race to the Top go to States that are leading the way with ambitious yet achievable plans for implementing coherent, compelling, and comprehensive education reform."[43]

Veteran teachers might critique the four areas above as follows:

> Numeral 1: Adopting standards and assessments? There are no shortages of either. No set of standards—no matter how well intentioned, and no tests, no matter how well developed, can make up for the lack of funding in the schools that score low on the tests or the dangerous circumstances and opportunity deprivation in which many low-income students must live.
>
> Numeral 2: Teachers and principals already know how to measure student success; no additional data systems are needed. Teachers and principals also know how to improve instruction, and that begins with making certain, for example, that each student has eaten that day and will have food over the weekend.
>
> Numeral 3: It is not an easy task to recruit and retain teachers in schools where they are needed—presumably the underfunded schools. Where are the willing teachers who can overlook filthy buildings, lack of materials, rodents, and other staples of underfunded schools? Some people won't even drive through the neighborhoods where these schools are located—and that's in the daylight. Who is going to "reward" these teachers and principals? What do they get—a plaque?
>
> Numeral 4: See Numerals 2 and 3.

EVERY STUDENT SUCCEEDS ACT

The most recent federal education act, the Every Student Succeeds Act[44] (ESSA), was signed into law at the end of 2015. The ESSA has been seen as less "prescriptive" than No Child Left Behind, but "annual statewide assessments" of "high academic standards" are "highlights" in the law as is the "expectation that there will be accountability and action to effect positive change in our lowest-performing schools."[45]

Redbud Elementary School, with its D and F ratings, is one of those schools. Without ameliorating the difficulties discussed in the previous chapters of this book, hope fades that the ESSA will be more successful than previous laws. ESSA does emphasize investments in access to "high-quality" preschools—an admirable highlight.

Johnson and Pratt-Johnson[46] told a tale of two New York City locations: One location is a private school where tuition is $26,000 per year, mornings only, for 2-year-olds. The rooms in the school are filled with children's books, age-appropriate art supplies, costly sets of building blocks, puppets, and more. Activities completed each day are posted on the window near the entrance. There are age-appropriate Spanish lessons, art discussions, cooking classes, little gardening projects—all taught by specialists (e.g., Ms. Cassie, the art teacher; Mr. James, the Spanish teacher; Ralph the chef).

In contrast to the private school environment is a soup kitchen in Brooklyn where Johnson and Pratt-Johnson volunteered as tray bussers. They told about a child, about 2 years old, in a stroller, who was parked at a table one day among a small group of "guests"—those who were eating the free lunch. No one spoke to the child for the duration of the lunch time. There was no story from an attractive children's book; there was no planting of seeds in a little decorative pot; there was no cooking class; there was no art lesson.

There were periodic warnings from the "woman in charge" of the soup kitchen when guests became rowdy and shouted insults to others. The children who attend the private school will have a head start when they go to preschool. The child at the soup kitchen was learning, too, but it entailed vocabulary that surely differed from the words and tones used by Ms. Cassie, Mr. James, and Chef Ralph.

TEACHING IS NOT FOR EVERYONE

"Ignorant clod pates" was how one novice teacher described her students. When she lost her patience with two pupils and called them "dunces," she was fired. Another beginning teacher resigned after 2 months because "the nervous strain was too much for me." An educator who decided to stay with the job said that "it is very hard work," that she had to accommodate "every level of learning," and when she received her pay, it was "highly discouraging . . . nothing beyond . . . subsistence."

The three teachers above lived during the Civil War era; their comments are recorded by Faust.[47] Sarah Morgan (1842–1909), a wealthy Louisiana diarist who wrote throughout the Civil War, admitted:

> I would rather die than teach. . . . My soul revolts from the drudgery. . . . I never see a governess that my heart does not ache for her. I think of the nameless, numberless, insults and trials she is forced to submit to; of the hopeless, thankless task that is imposed on her, to which she is expected to submit with out [sic] a murmur.[48]

"It was the worst week of my life," a beginning New York City teacher reported more recently when describing his first week on-the-job. He had been assigned to an unruly classroom of high school students. The novice educator left teaching and took a more lucrative and less nerve-wracking job selling medical instruments to hospitals.[49]

Labaree wrote that "teaching is an enormously difficult job that looks easy."[50] Many parents who helped their children with schoolwork during the COVID-19 outbreaks learned this rather quickly. Teachers work with many students each day—not just one or a few—and as pointed out in previous chapters, curriculum delivery is only one part of their days; when students are repeatedly absent from class, teachers are expected to "catch them up" on what they missed while gone. School report cards do not take such cases into account.

Teachers know that not all students want to be in school. It is not viewed by some in society as a desirable place to be, and even young children pick up on this notion. Local television weather forecasters, for example, might be heard saying, "Your kids will be happy today! No school in our viewing region!" Some might be glad that classes are cancelled and see it as a lucky occurrence, but those students who rely on free breakfast and free lunch know that they will be hungry on no-school days.

In some schools, educators are witnesses to or victims of violent acts. The statistics stun. As of this writing, the most recent data (i.e., 2016–2017) from the National Center for Education Statistics showed that 1.4 million crimes had been committed at schools, including physical attacks, fights, and thefts. During that time, 10% of teachers were threatened with injury from students.[51]

Tornay reported "screaming at teachers, throwing objects ranging from musical instruments to chairs, and leaving class without permission but with loud outbursts"[52] among the behaviors of students. There is a reason why the American Psychological Association published the brochure "A Silent National Crisis: Violence Against Teachers."[53]

Personal accounts bring tangibility to numbers. A high school teacher in an urban school recalled:

> Gangs are a very real problem in our district and added to the fighting that went on in the school. Whenever a fight took place in the school (and there were many), 80 percent of the student body would run through the halls to follow the fight. From outside the building, all you heard was the roar.
>
> During those altercations, when students barreled through the halls, teachers were supposed to stand against the walls. I, being a new teacher at the time, didn't realize the protocol and found myself being carried and trampled upon (up a stairway) during one of those events. Fortunately, another teacher nearby was able to grab my hand to pull me out and against the wall.[54]

School shootings have necessitated lessons in teacher and student preparedness. These realities are not mentioned when education critics engage in the tired "summers and holidays off" routine.

THE TEACHER SHORTAGE

As the number of students of color in the schools has increased, the racial component of the teaching force has remained static; most teachers are White. Classroom teachers, ideally, should be more racially diverse so that their students can see themselves in those who lead the class. Yet why should university students of color pursue a teaching degree? In the past, racism barred—at least covertly—students from entering some professions other than teaching.

These days, as Gray pointed out, "It's not seen as the ideal career to have, and so therefore our youngsters, our black children tend to move in other directions."[55] Students of color are not the only demographic that is dismissing teaching as a career. In the past decade, 340,000 fewer students chose to seek a degree in education; some states saw a 50% decrease in the number of education majors, and others saw even larger percentages.[56]

Taylor stated, "We have to look at professionalizing teachers and giving them a better work environment. . . . At some point even if you have a great teacher and you pay them an OK salary, they're still going to get burned out because of all the red tape and hoops they have to go through."[57] Prospective teachers start early on dealing with red tape and hoops, and these hurdles begin with testing.

States require various tests to become a certified teacher. There are content tests, each costing money. The students presumably already know the content; they've been studying it for years as undergraduates, and one would assume that their university professors would not give blanket grades of A to their students. Some of the tests are given in locales that require transportation to those sites. That, too, costs dollars. Any test retakes and time off from a job to take these retakes add to the bill. In addition to state-mandated tests, there's a relatively new player in teacher preparation: edTPA.

A visit to the edTPA website provided details about the assessment, which, in part, requires teacher candidates to submit lesson plans and classroom video recordings that are reviewed and scored by personnel other than the candidates' education professors. A page from the site, "About edTPA," stated, "edTPA is a performance-based, subject-specific assessment and support system used by teacher preparation programs throughout the United States to emphasize, measure and support the skills and knowledge that all teachers need from Day 1 in the classroom."[58]

The "Day 1" notion was reiterated in an AACTE (American Association of Colleges for Teacher Education) press release[59] that carried the subtitle: "edTPA Helps Determine Whether Aspiring Teachers are [sic] Ready to Teach From Day One." As with other professions/occupations, those entering a classroom on "Day 1" most likely will encounter episodes that no canned video or detailed lesson plans and assessments could predict. Teaching is too spontaneous; circumstances are too unpredictable. A child's dog died the previous evening; a mother was hospitalized; the rent money ran out.

As Jackson wrote, "The *immediacy* of classroom events is something that anyone who has ever been in charge of a roomful of students can never forget."[60] There are innumerable interactions with students that cannot be planned regardless of the assessment students had to complete in their undergraduate years. How can one plan for 1,000 interpersonal interchanges per school day in the lower grades and interpersonal interactions with approximately 150 students of varying needs and abilities in the upper grades?[61]

A senior education major in the state of New York pointed out the costs involved in seeking a degree in the field. The student stated, "My education costs a lot more than just tuition." She referred to transportation needed to get to off-campus practica and paying for mandatory tests such as the edTPA. "Education programs are set up for people who come from a certain position of privilege—that could keep a lot of people from entering the field."[62]

In an article that discussed the loss of students in teacher preparation programs, two students, whose career plans changed from teaching to political science and public administration, explained their reasons for the switch. One noted the "certification snafu (dealing with a controversial state rollout of edTPA), rigid Common Core standards, ramped-up teacher performance reviews and an over-reliance on testing." A second student mentioned being "increasingly turned off by the thought of teaching to the formulaic Common Core."[63]

Mills, in examining why fewer students are choosing teaching as a career, highlighted a teacher who came from a family of educators. The teacher noted that "how we're being held accountable" is a factor in students opting out of teaching and in teachers leaving the profession before retirement. It's the *how* that seems to matter to educators. The interviewee mentioned that the accountability factor "goes into making decisions about what curriculum you teach, how you approach students who need additional support. . . . It feels more and more that teachers have less say in what they get to do."[64]

A quotation from Duke, who saw his university's enrollment in the teacher education program decrease 49% in 7 years, seems appropriate at this juncture: "We have made it flat-out unattractive to be a teacher."[65]

TEACHER EDUCATORS

Those who teach students who aspire to be educators have not been exempt from accountability mandates. State departments of education and teacher education accreditors add to the demands of teaching, research, and service in which professors must engage. Enormous amounts of time can be spent in making syllabi uniform—despite the obvious violations to academic freedom.

Professors' keying and coding of standards and their elements are expected by those who inspect the programs of schools and colleges of education. In some states, passing accreditors' reviews, such as those conducted by Council for the Accreditation of Educator Preparation (CAEP), are mandatory. Although some professors have bought into the time and money spent on additional accreditation, others see it as nothing but busywork. Many ask, and rightfully so, "Where is the evidence that those who attend a school with this 'special' accreditation are better teachers—by any description—than those who do not graduate from such a program?"

Among interviews conducted by Johnson and colleagues, a respondent in a science department, who volunteered to help his teacher-education colleagues meet an accreditor's demand for multidisciplinary data, wrote:

> We try to develop a culture of discovery—of impassioned inquiry in our field. We can't pigeonhole students in the same mold.... We resent being told how to do our business with its [i.e., the accreditor's] bureaucratic, top-down mold.... We don't have time for this minutiae.... Their "rigor" amounts to nothing more than bean counting.[66]

Those beans can be costly in terms of dollars for workshops, perhaps consultants, and other preps for an accreditor's review. The beans are also expensive in terms of faculty time. The ultimate cost could be the loss of a university's teacher education accreditation if such accreditation is required by the state.

Education professors who are responsible for helping students pass assessments, such as the edTPA, might find themselves teaching to the assessment—not unlike classroom teachers relegated to teaching to a standardized test. Madeloni and Gorlewski pointed out that even valuable components of a teacher education program, such as student teaching seminars where real-life issues are discussed, might be reduced to working on edTPA completion.[67]

LOW PAY

Teacher walkouts in recent years underscore the difficulties many educators have in earning a living on just their salaries. According to one survey, 59% of teachers work a second job for financial reasons.[68] *TIME* magazine ran a cover story on the problem, citing in the corresponding article that a teacher in Kentucky had to take a sick day because she lacked the gas to drive to school.[69] The pay gap, the article noted, between educators and other professionals with comparable educations is "now the largest on record."[70]

THE WEEK[71] carried a brief section on 300–400 square feet "homes" being constructed in Arizona for teachers because they couldn't afford standard-size houses. It is not difficult to determine why so many university students, based solely on future income, shy away from becoming teachers. One teacher said, "My younger brother who's an engineer—his bonus is more than my salary."[72]

Until the value of what teachers do is appreciated, and until teachers cease to be paid mainly by local tax revenue, and until the country runs low on teachers who teach from the soul, and until the politics of the nation supports teachers, the sorry state of low teacher pay will continue.

WHAT DO TEACHERS DO?

The answer to the question above depends on where the educators teach. Those in underfunded public-school districts might act as launderers of student clothing, weekend meal providers, uncertified social workers and school psychologists, unlicensed medical personnel for minor injuries and illnesses, Samaritans who hand out self-purchased needed supplies, and makeshift thrift-store personnel. When a school, and that usually is a school that serves low-income families, is threatened with a takeover, the implication is that something is wrong with the adult personnel in the buildings.

As the Redbud story illustrates, this implicative blaming is erroneous. Conditions at home and in neighborhoods, lack of proper nutrition, inadequate medical and dental care, student and teacher turnover, all contribute to low test scores. The dedicated, selfless educators who work in low-income schools provide the stability that many students lack at home; they understand the toll that poverty takes on their students, and yet they choose to stay and help. Most could find more lucrative, less stressful teaching positions in higher-income neighborhoods. They need support, in all regards, not disparagement and threats.

WHAT SHOULD TEACHERS TEACH?

Curricular decisions have been a contentious subject throughout the history of public schools. Some subjects, such as reading and math, have been standard components of school study over the years. A 1861 report on subjects taught in the State of Nebraska, across grade levels, shows the following curricular components: alphabet (for younger pupils), orthography, reading, penmanship, natural philosophy, chemistry, physiology, English grammar, composition, rhetoric, vocal music, astronomy, bookkeeping, mental arithmetic, written arithmetic, algebra, geography, history, Latin.[73]

Religion is missing from the 1861 list, but those who want religion in the schools have been expressing their interests for a long time. Dr. William Mayo, of Mayo Clinic fame, was a school board member in Rochester, Minnesota, in 1867. Mayo believed that science "would free the world of misery and ignorance."[74] This stance put him at odds with those who dismissed Darwin's theory of evolution, and the name-calling by citizens opposed to Mayo's beliefs began. School board elections have been and continue to be important, because there are those who believe that Earth is flat and that dinosaurs are fictitious.

"What is rain for? What makes some flowers wild and some 'tame'? How do fruits that grow on farms reach the city? What is sleet? How is peanut butter made? What are the differences between whole wheat flour, graham flour, and white flour? Why does a finger bleed when pricked?"

"We wish to:

Improve our art work	Have class meetings
Learn to sing new songs	Make work aprons
Have a story-hour club	Learn to cook
Take a trip to the wholesale market	Study geography
Read many books	Make candles
Study history	Paint pictures
Write stories	Give a play
Work with wood	Have a class newspaper
Learn more about science	Make a book telling about our city
Improve our arithmetic	Make tiles of clay
Make a yearbook	Have a picnic in the country"

The set of questions above were generated by kindergarten pupils during two class meetings. A class of third graders listed the topics that follow the questions as goals for their school year. The children's questions and plans are included in the third volume of *The Classroom Teacher*. The copyright date is 1927–1928. The authors of the volume—Moore, Betzner, and Lewis—stated:

> Children like to ask how and why. They like to try a thing out to see what will happen. . . . This clearly suggests that the activities embodied in the [classroom] work should include much that is experimental, investigative, exploratory. . . . Watching to see what happens is much better than listening to someone's discussion of what happened, and being the cause of what happens gives a genuine satisfaction in the activity. This satisfaction is the finest of spurs to further activity.[75]

The change in elementary school curriculum from the late 1920s to today reflects a lack of trust in educators—those who work with children and, other than their parents and guardians, know the pupils best. The sea change can best be summed up in words by a teacher in Missouri: "When I started teaching in the late 1990s, teachers were not seen as idiots who couldn't be trusted. We weren't viewed as evil and lazy like we are now."[76] If teachers weren't viewed as incompetent, why would publishers sell scripted "teacher-proof" lessons? Someone who holds the purse strings is buying them.

Katz wrote:

> Even people who have been willing to accept a poor salary and who can remain indifferent to status have been repelled by the lack of autonomy, the rigid and petty authoritarian ethos of the schools. Bright, creative, and well-educated people want to function as professionals, to make the decisions about how they will do their job. Education has not suffered from any freedom granted teachers to run schools as they see fit; it has suffered from the suffocating atmosphere in which teachers have had to work.[77]

Katz's statements were published in 1971—before NCLB, high-stakes testing, school report cards, and other phenomena attached to "accountability."

Businessman and philanthropist David Longaberger was one of 12 children who stocked shelves at the age of 6 and built a business into a $700-million-a-year enterprise that employed 7,000 people and 47,000 salespeople.[78] Longaberger recognized the vital role that those who have first-hand experience can play. He said:

> I truly believe that the world's best source of information about any business is the people who spend eight hours a day working there. Big companies spend huge fees to bring in consultants, when all the answers (and the right answers at that) are available for free. All they have to do is listen to their employees.[79]

Jackson discussed interviews with teachers that occurred before the standards/accountability movement was in full force. An inflexible curriculum, one that frowned upon teaching material outside the prescribed lessons, aroused strong responses from the interviewees. One teacher said,

> If I were given a curriculum guide and a series of lesson plans that said "You will teach this way; you will teach this material at this time and take so long to do it," if they made teaching too rigid or started telling me that I must use this book or that book and could not bring in supplementary materials of my own, and then I'd quit. Forget it! You can hire an orangutan to come in and pass out books. You really can! I'd walk out the door tomorrow.[80]

Other teachers responded similarly to the notion of having guidelines in place that do not respect their professional wisdom and knowledge about what is appropriate for their students.

As noted earlier, *A Nation at Risk* was published in 1983; No Child Left Behind was signed into law in 2002. The biographies of American Nobel Prize winners, who attended public schools prior to these events, illustrated what American teachers can do for students when they are allowed to be educators.

> F. Sherwood Rowland (The Nobel Prize in Chemistry, 1995): "All of my elementary and high school education was received in the Delaware [Ohio] public schools from an excellent set of teachers. . . . In several summers of my early teens, the high school science teacher entrusted to me during his two week vacations the operation of the local volunteer weather station, an auxiliary part of the U.S. weather service-maximum and minimum temperatures and total precipitation. This was my first exposure to systematic experimentation and data collection."[81]

Edwin G. Krebs received the Nobel Prize in Physiology or Medicine in 1992. Krebs recalled:

> In the period from 1933 to 1940 in Urbana [Illinois] I completed the last three years of high school and carried out undergraduate work at the University of Illinois. Urbana High School was an excellent institution with highly dedicated teachers and a broad range of extracurricular activities that were useful in helping me make up my mind as to what I wanted to do in life. . . . In 1936, I entered the University of Illinois with the idea of majoring in some branch of science related to chemistry, but I did not have a very clear idea of where I was headed. Taking advantage of an "individual curriculum" program. . . . I was relieved of the necessity of meeting many specific requirements and could pick and choose courses that I wanted.[82]

The Nobel laureates above and others attended public schools when no national curriculum was imposed. The absence of "rigorous" standards, teaching to the test, and reading scripts for instruction did not seem to harm the recipients' careers.

Perhaps most people would agree that cultivating a creative mind, one that advances the human condition in various ways to alleviate suffering and make life more intrinsically rewarding, would be a worthwhile endeavor for educators and their charges to pursue. What contributes to an inventive mind? A parent can play a role.

McCullough wrote that Susan Koerner Wright, mother of Wilbur and Orville, with her aptitude for mechanics, could build "anything." Their father believed that toys had educational value. McCullough noted that Orville Wright's first-grade teacher saw him tinker at his desk; the materials with which he tinkered were to be combined for a model of a flying machine.[83] There is little time for tinkering when test scores are used to determine a school's ranking.

WHAT TYPE OF CURRICULUM BUILDS AND SUPPORTS INVENTIVE MINDS?

Most people would agree that science education is vital to our country's future in all regards. The need for top-notch scientific investigators was underscored when the COVID-19 pandemic hit. It is likely, however, that many citizens are not aware of what has happened to science education in elementary schools.

If taught at all, science is relegated to the back burners in a school week that is focused on reading and mathematics. When the subject is taught, some teachers have reported that it is done as an afterthought because it is not being tested. Science has been relegated to the "fluff" category of curriculum as seen in the tale of Redbud Elementary School.

Thomas Edison said, "To invent, you need a good imagination and a pile of junk."[84] Physicist Max Born noted, "Science is not formal logic—it needs the free play of the mind in as great a degree as any other creative art."[85]

Farenga and colleagues echoed Edison and Born's sentiments in their observations of young children at play. They pointed out that a problem with contemporary science instruction—if that instruction exists at all—is a structure that is too rigid. The authors wrote that under such rigidity, "The answers are structured to fit course assessments, and the wonder of science is lost along with cognitive intrigue."[86]

If scientists at the National Aeronautics and Space Administration (NASA) were disguised as classroom teachers, they might have a difficult time justifying a component of their curriculum to adherents of the accountability movement, because NASA teachers might take students outdoors to construct and then fly kites. On NASA's webpage "Welcome to the Beginner's Guide to Kites,"[87] NASA stated:

> An excellent way for students to gain an understanding and a feel for many of the concepts that they learn in math and physics is to build and fly a kite. The forces on a kite are so similar to the forces on an airplane that the Wright brothers often flew their gliders as tethered kites to determine the aerodynamic characteristics. Like an airplane, a kite is heavier than air and relies on the motion of the wind past the kite to generate the aerodynamic lift necessary to overcome the weight of the kite. The movement of the air past the kite also generates aerodynamic drag which is overcome by constraining the kite with a control line. The interaction of these forces determines the overall performance which varies with the design of the kite.

NASA included a "Kite Index" on its site that listed topics covered in kite construction and flying. The index list was lengthy, but some topics included: area, volume, vector components, forces on a kite, balance and stability, determining flight altitude, air pressure and temperature, and kite safety.

TEACHERS AND AMERICA'S FUTURE

What are the ramifications of the changes in teachers' roles and in curricula from what the country did in the late 1920s to the present? How could these changes impact our nation's competitive future? Since the kindergartners asked their questions and the third graders made their list until the NCLB Act was signed in 2002, American inventors have given us the artificial heart, nylon, laundromats, parking meters, helicopters, chocolate chip cookies, radar, microwave ovens, the polio vaccine, the calculator, lasers,[88] and enough consumer tech devices to fill another chapter in this volume.

Few would suggest that students make puppets or fly kites all day every day. Transferable skills, such as learning to decode words, must be learned in classrooms, and teacher-selected periodic tests on these skills are warranted. Standardized tests can inform with relevant data, but they should not be the tools that determine the fate of pupils, their teachers, and their schools. Madaus said it best:

> The long-term negative effects on curriculum, teaching, and learning of using measurement as the engine, or primary motivating power of the educational process, outweigh those positive benefits attributed to it. The tests can become the ferocious master of the educational process, not the compliant servant they should be.[89]

A good dose of freedom to think and to create should be a part of curricula at all levels. Teachers, if they are to educate and inspire, need the space to function as the remarkable professionals that they are. Teaching involves artistry, and just as no serious visual artist would produce and exhibit paint-by-the-numbers "works" on canvasses, no serious teacher should be held to paint-by-the-numbers demands under which so many must work.

NOTES

1. Otto L. Bettmann, *The Good Old Days—They Were Terrible!* (New York: Random House, 1974), 162.

2. Michael B. Katz, *Class, Bureaucracy, & Schools: The Illusion of Educational Change in America* (New York: Praeger, 1971), 131.

3. Claudia Levin (Producer, Director), Meg Pinto (Associate Producer, Scriptwriter), Charles Scott (Editor), Stephen McCarthy (Cinematographer), and Allen Moore (Cinematographer), *Only a Teacher* [Television Series/Video], accessed May 28, 2020, http://pbs.org/onlyateacher.

4. Donald Pfanz, *Clara Barton's Civil War* (Yardley, PA: Westholme Publishing, 2018).

5. University of Northern Iowa, "History and Traditions," accessed April 21, 2020, https://uni.edu/resources/history-traditions.

6. University of California, Los Angeles, "State Normal School Opens in Los Angeles," accessed April 21, 2020, https://alumni.gseis.ucla.edu/?timeline=state-normal-school-opens-in-los-angeles.

7. Bettmann, *The Good Old Days*, 168.

8. Everett Dick, *The Sod-House Frontier: 1854-1890* (Lincoln, NE: Johnsen Publishing Company, 1954), 323.

9. Marta McDowell, *The World of Laura Ingalls Wilder: The Frontier Landscapes that Inspired the Little House Books* (Portland, OR: Timber Press, 2017), 184.

10. Bettmann, *The Good Old Days*, 158.

11. Dick, *The Sod-House Frontier*, 324.

12. See Bonnie Johnson and Yvonne Pratt-Johnson, "Factors Behind the Digital Divide," in *Inequalities in the Early Years*, eds. Bonnie Johnson and Yvonne Pratt-Johnson (New York: Routledge, 2018), 3.

13. Louis Menand, *The Metaphysical Club: A Story of Ideas in America* (New York: Farrar, Straus, and Giroux, 2001), 323.

14. Eisenhower Presidential Library, "Quotes," accessed April 17, 2020, http://eisenhowerlibrary.gov/eisenhowers/quotes.

15. U.S. House of Representatives, "National Defense Education Act," https://history.house.gov/Records-and-Research/Listing/lfp_006.

16. The third-grade teacher is the author of this volume.

17. National Commission on Excellence in Education, *A Nation at Risk: The Imperative for Educational Reform* (Washington, DC: US Government Printing Office, 1983), accessed April 20, 2020, ww2.ed.gov/pubs/NatAtRisk/members.html.

18. Ibid., 1.

19. Dale D. Johnson, Bonnie Johnson, Stephen J. Farenga, and Daniel Ness, *Trivializing Teacher Education: The Accreditation Squeeze* (Lanham, MD: Rowman & Littlefield, 2005), 94–95.

20. NCATE, the National Council for Accreditation of Teacher Education, has been supplanted by other accreditors such as CAEP (Council for the Accreditation of Educator Preparation), which has its own set of standards.

21. The International Reading Association is now the International Literacy Association.

22. The author of this volume has heard numerous firsthand reports of such activities from her graduate students who are classroom teachers.

23. National Commission on Excellence in Education, *A Nation at Risk*, 5.

24. Dale D. Johnson and Bonnie Johnson, *High Stakes: Poverty, Testing, and Failure in American Schools*, 2nd ed. (Lanham, MD: Rowman & Littlefield, 2006), 197.

25. Bonnie Johnson, "Every Day She Drunk or Gone," in *Alternatives to Privatizing Public Education and Curriculum: A Festschrift in Honor of Dale D. Johnson*, eds. Daniel Ness and Stephen J. Farenga (New York: Routledge, 2017), 169–188.

26. Ibid.

27. National Commission on Excellence in Education, *A Nation at Risk*, 2.

28. Johnson, "Every Day She Drunk or Gone," 180.

29. Michael Apple, Foreword, in *Trivializing Teacher Education: The Accreditation Squeeze* (Lanham, MD: Rowman & Littlefield, 2005), xiii.

30. April Hall, "Beyond the Noise," *Reading Today* 32, no. 3 (November/December 2014): 18–25.

31. P. David Pearson, quoted in Hall, "Beyond the Noise," 20.

32. Ibid., 20.

33. Valerie Strauss, "Teacher Slams Scripted Common Core Lessons That Must Be Taught 'Word for Word,'" *Washington Post*, November 30, 2013, www.washingtonpost.com/news/answer-sheet/wp/2013/11/30/teacher-slams-scripted-common-core-lessons-that-must-be-taught-word-for-word.

34. Personal communication to Dale D. Johnson and the author of this volume, 2013.

35. For a more complete discussion on the topic, see Bonnie Johnson and Yvonne Pratt-Johnson, "Early Literacy: Home, School, Neighborhood," in *What's Hot in Literacy: Exemplar Models of Effective Practice*, eds. Evan Ortlieb, Stephanie Grote-Garcia, Jack Cassidy, and Earl H. Cheek Jr. (Bingley, UK: Emerald Publishing, 2020), 33–50.

36. Dale D. Johnson, Bonnie Johnson, Stephen J. Farenga, and Daniel Ness, *Stop High-Stakes Testing* (Lanham, MD: Rowman & Littlefield, 2008), 17–18.

37. Natalie Wexler, "The Radical Case for Teaching Kids Stuff," *The Atlantic* 324, no. 2 (August 2019), 22.

38. Eleanor Duckworth, quoted in Elaine McArdle, "What Happened to the Common Core?" *Harvard Ed. Magazine*, Fall 2014, www.gse.harvard.edu/news/ed/14/09/what-happened-common-core.

39. Chris Buttimer, quoted in McArdle, "What Happened to the Common Core?"

40. Ibid.

41. Mariana Souto-Manning, "The Teaching Profession Provides Little Room for Growth," *New York Times*, September 11, 2014, http://nytimes.com/roomfordebate/2014/09/11/how-to-diversify-teaching/the-teaching-profession-provides-little-room-for-growth.

42. Race to the Top Fund, "Program Description," accessed June 2, 2020, www2.ed.gov/programs/racetothetop/index.html.

43. Ibid.

44. U.S. Department of Education, "Every Student Succeeds Act (ESSA)," accessed June 21, 2021, http://ed.gov/essa?src=rn.

45. Ibid.

46. Johnson and Pratt-Johnson, "Factors Behind the Digital Divide."

47. Drew Gilpin Faust, *Mothers of Invention: Women of the Slaveholding South in the American Civil War* (Chapel Hill: The University of North Carolina Press, 1996), 87–88.

48. Sarah Morgan, *Sarah Morgan: The Civil War Diary of a Southern Woman*, ed. Charles East (New York: Simon & Schuster, 1991), 153.

49. The novice teacher is the brother of the author's former student.

50. David F. Labaree, *The Trouble with Ed Schools* (New Haven, CT: Yale University Press, 2004), 39.

51. National Center for Education Statistics, "School Crime," accessed May 17, 2020, https://nces.ed.gov/fastfacts/display.asp?id=49.

52. Kaylee Tornay, "Teachers, Parents Report Increase in Unruly Students," *Associated Press*, June 19, 2018, www.apnews.com/235024be3f984493b54aec8bfbdd2d4c.

53. Dorothy Espelage and Linda Reddy, "A Silent National Crisis: Violence Against Teachers," American Psychological Association, January 2016, http://apa.org/education/k12/teacher-victimization.

54. The teacher was Dale D. Johnson's graduate student and an acquaintance of the author.

55. LaRuth Gray, scholar-in-residence at the Metropolitan Center for Research on Equity and the Transformation of Schools at New York University, and government liaison for the National Alliance of Black School Educators, cited in Associated Press in Washington, "US Teachers Are Not Nearly as Diverse as Their Students, New Studies Say," *The Guardian*, May 5, 2014, www.theguardian.com/world/2014/may/05/us-teachers-diverse-students-new-studies.

56. Lauren Camera, "Sharp Nationwide Enrollment Drop in Teacher Prep Programs Cause for Alarm," *U.S. News & World Report*, December 3, 2019, www.usnews.com/news/education-news/articles/2019-12-03/sharp-nationwide-enrollment-drop-in-teacher-prep-programs-cause-for-alarm.

57. Jameson Taylor, quoted in Bracey Harris, "Financial Support for Public Schools—and Population—Are Shrinking in Mississippi. Is There an Easy Fix?" *Clarion Ledger*, February 26, 2019, www.mississippitoday.org/2019/02/26/financial-support-for-public-schools-and-population-are-shrinking-in-mississippi-is-there-an-easy-fix.

58. edTPA. "About edTPA," accessed May 26, 2020, www.edtpa.com/PageView.aspx?f=GEN_AboutEdTPA.html.

59. American Association of Colleges for Teacher Education, "New Assessment for Teacher Candidates Rolls Out after Two Years of Field Testing: edTPA Helps Determine Whether Aspiring Teachers are [*sic*] Ready to Teach from Day One," November 8, 2013, https://

aacte.org/2013/11/new-assessment-for-teacher-candidates-rolls-out-after-two-years-of-field-testing.

60. Philip W. Jackson, *Life in Classrooms* (New York: Teachers College Press, 1990), 119.

61. Thomas L. Good and Jere E. Brophy, *Looking in Classrooms*, 9th ed. (New York: Pearson, 2003), 23.

62. Kara Smith, "Southern Tier Educators Brainstorm Teacher Shortage Solutions," *NYSUT United*, May/June 2020, 17.

63. Darryl McGrath, "The Big Chill: Flawed Certification and Attacks on Public Education Cause Fewer Students to Choose Teaching as Profession. Unions Push for Solutions," *NYSUT United* 6, no. 1 (Fall 2015): 20.

64. Shamane Mills, "Why Are Fewer Wisconsin Students Studying to Become Teachers?" *WPR News*, February 5, 2019, www.wpr.org/why-are/fewer/wisconsin-students- studying-become-teachers.

65. Bryan Duke, quoted in Camera, "Sharp Nationwide Enrollment Drop."

66. Johnson et al., *Trivializing Teacher Education*, 39–40.

67. Barbara Madeloni and Julie Gorlewski, "Radical Imagination, Not Standardization: Critical Teacher Education and the edTPA," *Teachers College Record*, June 21, 2013, www.tcrecord.org/PrintContent.asp?ContentID=17163.

68. The survey was conducted by NPR and was noted in "The Teachers' Revolt," *THE WEEK*, June 1, 2018, 11.

69. Katie Reilly, "The Life of the American Teacher," *TIME*, September 24, 2018, 26 and cover.

70. Ibid., 28.

71. *THE WEEK*, "Only in America," August 17/24, 2018, 6.

72. Reilly, "The Life of the American Teacher," 33.

73. Dick, *The Sod-House Frontier*, 321.

74. Sister Ellen Whelan, *The Sisters' Story: Saint Marys Hospital—Mayo Clinic 1889–1939* (Rochester, MN: Mayo Foundation for Medical Education and Research, 2002), 12–13.

75. Annie E. Moore, Jean Betzner, and Mary Lewis, *The Classroom Teacher*, vol. 3 (Chicago: The Classroom Teacher Inc., 1927–1928), 13–14, 486.

76. Bridgett Blake, quoted in Alexandra Robbins, "Teachers Deserve More Respect," *New York Times*, March 22, 2020, 7.

77. Katz, *Class, Bureaucracy, & Schools*, 131.

78. Dave Longaberger, *Longaberger: An American Success Story* (New York: HarperBusiness, 2001); Robert Thomas Jr., "David Longaberger, Basket Maker, Dies at 64," *New York Times*, March 22, 1999, www.nytimes.com/1999/03/22/us/david-longaberger-basket-maker-dies-at-64.html.

79. Longaberger, *Longaberger*, 49.

80. Jackson, *Life in Classrooms*, 129.

81. The Nobel Prize, "F. Sherwood Rowland," Accessed May 31, 2020, http://nobelprize.org/prizes/chemistry/1995/Rowland/biographical.

82. The Nobel Prize. "Edwin G. Krebs," 1992, http://nobelprize.org/prizes/medicine/1992/krebs/biographical.

83. David McCullough, *The Wright Brothers* (New York: Simon & Schuster, 2015), 1, 10.

84. Thomas Edison, "'To invent, you need a good imagination and a pile of junk.'" Smithsonian Libraries, February 11, 2011, http://blog.library.si.edu/blog/2011/02/11/to-invent-you-need-a-good-imagination-and-a-pile-of-junk.

85. Max Born, quoted in Carol Kelly-Gangi, ed., *The Essential Wisdom of the World's Greatest Thinkers* (New York: Fall River Press, 2016), 74.

86. Stephen J. Farenga, Daniel Ness, Bonnie Johnson, and Dale D. Johnson, *The Importance of Average* (Lanham, MD: Rowman & Littlefield, 2010), 125.

87. National Aeronautics and Space Administration, "Welcome to the Beginner's Guide to Kites," accessed June 2, 2020, http://grc.nasa,gov/www/K-12/airplane/shortk.html.

88. Gorton Carruth, *What Happened When* (New York: Penguin, 1989).

89. George F. Madaus, "The Influence of Testing on the Curriculum," in *Issues in Curriculum: Selected Chapters from NSSE Yearbooks*, eds. Margaret J. Early and Kenneth J. Rehage (Chicago: The National Society for the Study of Education, 1999), 74–75.

Chapter Nine

Some Costs of Poverty and Glimmers of Hope

"WHY ARE PEOPLE POOR?"

"Anyone who has ever struggled with poverty knows how extremely expensive it is to be poor," wrote James Baldwin in 1961.[1] The costs of poverty are evident from the early years through adulthood. Closed-minded, harsh attitudes toward economically poor individuals can form at a young age. In a survey of financially privileged middle-schoolers from Long Island, New York, Johnson and colleagues[2] received the following answers to the questions, "Why are people poor?" "What are the causes of poverty?"

> Jake, seventh grader: "Because they make poor decisions. They often come from bad families or broken homes. A lot of the time they are lazy."
> Valerie, sixth grader: "Because they don't work hard."
> Chase, eighth grader: "There is a lot of poverty in the world, and I strongly believe that the main reason is that people do not work hard enough, they are lazy and do not have the motivation to better themselves."
> Lynn, tenth grader: "Because they are too lazy to get off their butts and get a job. . . . They caused it because if they really cared about being poor, then they would get a job."
> Summer, eighth grader: "I believe people are poor because of laziness."

None of the respondents mentioned unexpected illnesses or job losses, low wages, discriminatory racial- or class-based practices, or any other explanations for being poor. The interviewees had not even entered high school, but they already had learned to blanket-blame the victims.

Johnson and colleagues found a sense of self-assurance among the interviewees—a certainty that their futures would be sunny. Nathan, for example, at age 13 stated:

> I am going to go to college; there has never been any other option for me. I have a lot of ambitions in life, and what I want to do with my life requires a college education. I do not know the exact college that I want to go to, but the college will be a prestigious one. I want to do something with business and law, the exact field I do not know, but my career will be in the realm of business and law.[3]

For most young people such as Nathan, the years ahead of them will be filled with opportunities; their parents would have it no other way. The same cannot be said for children of poverty. Not having adequate funds to support a family does not mean that the parents care less about their children. It means that they do not have the dollars for extras that might enrich their children's lives and give them advantages in school. A science teacher in an affluent school district aptly described the advantages that money can provide:

> You can't miss the students who travel. They wear the experience like people wear jewelry. What I mean is that you can easily notice the athletes in the class, and you can just as easily notice the children who have had worldly experiences based on their travels. Their language, their outlook on the world, and the complexity of their thoughts all come to light during class discussions. The ease with which children share where they've been and what they've seen is apparent. Travel is an outstanding opportunity and education in itself. Substituting a week of school to visit Hong Kong, Paris, or Rome is no loss because of the education that's gained from the first-hand travel experience. Besides, most students have the option of working with a tutor to make up any work they've missed.[4]

The memories of growing up with little money stick with people even after they have achieved financial security. A successful lawyer recalled a class school trip where she went hungry rather than attempt to eat a club sandwich because it came with toothpicks on the ends, and she did not know how to eat it. The lawyer said, "I didn't know much about the world, and I always was afraid of making a wrong move. . . . I think class is everything. . . . To me, being from an upper class is all about confidence."[5]

THE COSTS OF BEING HUNGRY

In 1977, *food insecure* appeared in the vernacular. The term means that one does not have reliable access to food or enough money to buy that food if it is available.[6] By 2006, the U.S. Department of Agriculture (USDA) introduced "ranges of severity of food security" from high food security to low and very low food security.

The Committee on National Statistics of the National Academies noted a distinction between food insecurity and hunger:

- "Food insecurity ... is a household-level economic and social condition of limited or uncertain access to adequate food.
- Hunger is an individual-level physiological condition that may result from food insecurity."[7]

Whatever one chooses to call the condition of not having enough to eat, the characteristics of people with very low food security are disturbing. For example, according to the USDA, 98% of people in the very-low-food-security range were worried that they would run out of food before they had money to buy more, 97% stated that recently purchased food did not last long and they didn't have funds to buy more, and 97% of adults had reduced meal size or skipped meals because of lack of funds.[8]

Children who must live in the very-low-food-security range witness these circumstances. There are times in their young lives when they must be told that there aren't any more groceries in the home and that there will not be until relief, in some form, arrives.

Hunger/food insecurity also extracts tolls on school-age children outside the home. There sometimes are indignities in schools—places where children should feel safe from degrading circumstances beyond their control. A third-grade teacher, for example, recalls a day when a school assistant called over the intercom that a child needed to pick up his free lunch tickets. His classmates wanted to know why he received free lunches when they had to pay. The teacher had to "cover" for the child as he slumped at his desk.[9]

Lunch shaming is a practice that has been prevalent enough to warrant a definition from the American Bar Association (ABA), the professional organization for lawyers and law students. The ABA stated:

> Broadly speaking, "lunch shaming" refers to the overt identification and stigmatization of any student who does not have money to buy a school meal. . . . The purpose of lunch shaming is to embarrass a student and parent(s) so that a school lunch debt is paid quickly, in turn reducing a school's financial burden.[10]

News reporters have told of hot lunches being thrown away and replaced with cold lunches for students who owed $15.00 or more for their meals.[11] Some schools have punished students for meal debts by stamping their hands or giving them chores.[12] In one school district, parents who owed money were threatened with placing their children in foster care.[13] Other humiliating episodes appear in the media from time to time. Ralph Waldo Emerson (1803–1832) said, "Poverty demoralizes,"[14] and this demoralization, through lunch shaming, can take root at a young age.

Districts must make up the money from their local funds when lunch debts are not paid—no federal funds can be used for this purpose. Charities and occasionally businesses will help ease the debt burden through contributions. If school districts—especially underfunded districts—were not under pressure to raise test scores and feel the need to spend large sums of money on test prep, perhaps they could help families out when they do not have the dollars for school lunches.

The effects of nutrition-related disorders, such as malnutrition, diabetes, and obesity, were examined by Stehling and Mangione.[15] They reported that poor childhood nutrition can result in higher risks of infections, impaired cognitive functions, stunted growth, anemia, and increased risks of fractures.

Children with Type 1 diabetes who come from low-income families might experience more complications because of lack of adequate medical attention. The high prices of fruits, vegetables, and whole grains are a factor in some parents' decisions to opt for larger quantities of inexpensive foods. These choices, based on dollars and cents, contribute to what Harrington[16] called being "fat with hunger, for that is what cheap foods do."

Food desert, a term that was first used in 1988,[17] is defined as an area "where people have limited access to a variety of healthy and affordable food."[18] Dutko and colleagues[19] wrote that whether in an urban or a rural area, food deserts are locations with higher poverty rates than other geographic locations. Families without the funds to own a vehicle or money for transportation out of the food deserts must shop in higher-priced stores with fewer food choices; overpriced "convenience stores" come to mind.

The COVID-19 crisis revealed how precarious many families' food supplies are when jobs are lost. News coverage of drive-thru food distribution sites showed parking lots with 14-deep vehicle lines; lines could be miles long.[20] Some school districts delivered prepackaged breakfasts and lunches to students during the summer months to those who qualified for free and reduced meals. Buses were used so that masked and gloved school workers could pass the food through bus windows.[21] The virus took a toll on high schoolers who had to take full-time jobs when parents contracted the infection.[22] Someone had to pay the bills.

COSTS OF POVERTY IN THE HOME

As stated earlier in this chapter and volume, a low income does not mean that parents in this socioeconomic stratum care less about their children. Anyone who has taught in middle- or high-income schools can relate tales of parental neglect in all its forms. When a parent or guardian is earning a minimum wage or less, or when parents or guardians must work more than one job to support their families, however, stress can be greater than for those who have ample funds.

Depression, sometimes related to losing one's job, can result in the unemployed spending less time with family members—even though the unemployed person usually has more free time.[23] Self-worth deteriorates, arguments among parents ensue, blame is assigned, and all family members suffer. When frequent arguments arise over money problems, little ears most likely hear at least some of these conflicts. Children are not immune to worry, and they can bring that worry to school, as was seen among some Redbud pupils.

Effects of job loss have been long recognized. Cottle reported that when adults who work outside the home become unemployed, physical and mental problems can occur within 14 days.[24] Cottle wrote:

> Insomnia, upset stomachs, ear and nasal infections, and all sorts of flu symptoms are reported almost at once and may strike any member of the family. Then there are the achy joints, back pains, and severe headaches felt by people, including children, who never have been sick a day in their lives. . . . Then there is the matter of psychological disturbances and outright mental illness that may be detected in any family member as a function of a father or mother being out of work for long periods of time.[25]

The COVID-19 virus revealed a digital divide that has existed for years; as Johnson and Pratt-Johnson noted, for some families, the choice has been data plan or dinner.[26] When buildings were shuttered, and schools had to move to online learning, approximately one-third of economically poor households with school-age children lacked a high-speed internet connection.[27] Some students had to rely on mobile phones to participate in school assignments.[28]

There were Internet providers and other businesses who donated Wi-Fi connections and laptops to those in need, and some school districts were able to give requisite electronic tools to students who did not have them at home.[29] It still was a game of catch-up, though, for children who had to learn to use the equipment as well as learn the curriculum. Prior to the spread of the virus, states were spending over $1.7 billion annually on standardized testing[30]; if only those dollars—or even a portion of those dollars—had been spent on ensuring that all students had the tools needed at home to work in a digital learning environment.

… Chapter 9

THE COSTS OF NEIGHBORHOOD POVERTY

The *Mayo Clinic Family Health Book* listed emotional comfort among factors that affect a child's learning: "If a child is depressed, worried, or concerned about problems at home, learning can suffer."[31] Problems in the home such as drug abuse and physical altercations were conversation topics among Redbud pupils as the problems spilled into the neighborhood.

The Redbud teachers advised any newcomers that it was not safe to be in the area after 5:00 p.m. Pupils reported keeping late hours because, at times, the neighborhood was too noisy to sleep. An armed robbery at a local grocery store, where employees were forced into the cooler, was the main conversation topic one morning.

Emotional comfort, for some children, can be found at school. The classroom environment is predictable and safe. Pupils are among caring adults who make certain that the children are fed and protected. When those who have no experience in a school such as Redbud talk about taking over a failing school and moving the teachers out, they are suggesting a simplistic solution for a complex problem.

Johnson and colleagues wrote that to remove personnel from schools such as Redbud

> disparages the many exceptional teachers and administrators who work in such schools. More often than not, it is these selfless, experienced educators who provide the stability necessary in any school. These veteran teachers and administrators understand the problems associated with poverty.[32]

The Children's Defense Fund reported that children are the poorest age group in America, and that childhood poverty is "unnecessary, costly and the greatest threat to the nation's future national, economic, and military security."[33] Those politicians and policymakers, who claim to be concerned about the country's future, need to understand that investing in failing schools makes more sense than berating these schools.

GLIMMERS OF HOPE

Anthropologist Margaret Mead stated, "Never doubt that a small group of thoughtful committed citizens can change the world. In fact, it's the only thing that ever has."[34] Although government planning and implementation grants—such as the Promise Neighborhoods program,[35] a provision of the Every Student Succeeds Act—have been available, completing a grant application takes time and proficiency with the process.

There are grassroots efforts, however, that work to improve the lives of students. The programs have various names such sunrise-to-sunset schools[36] and community schools,[37] where a variety of services are offered that go beyond the traditional curriculum.

Some efforts are small in scale but can be large in importance in a child's life. The Back to School Store[38] for elementary and middle school children in a small Midwestern community is such an effort. At the store, students can select a back-to-school outfit, shoes, socks, underclothing, and a backpack filled with school supplies that are on their schools' required supplies lists—all free of charge.

While at the store, accompanying adults learn about childhood nutrition and safety. The store survives on donations and volunteers. It's a once-a-year event, but it at least gives pupils the supplies that they need to start school, and they can do so with shoes that fit. Vision and dental screenings also are provided at the store.

Dollars from the New York State United Teachers and the American Federation of Teachers have helped to establish programs such as "the People Project," which invests in "community dinners, food pantries, backpack food projects, food trucks, clothes closets, book giveaways, transportation to school events, and...after-school and summer care programs."[39]

Another effort in central New York, funded by the American Federation of Teachers, established community schools where school-based staff help families get "dental care, mental health care, food and housing."[40] These community schools also provide family computer labs, parenting classes, and summer programs for students. With teachers at the helm and teachers' dues providing the money, red tape is reduced, and so are the "visions" and demands of those who never worked a day with economically poor children and their families.

Several years ago, a teacher in a Long Island school that served mostly economically poor children wrote about her students and their years ahead. Her words below are a fitting conclusion to this volume:

> We have a new superintendent at my school, and he said that our children are equal to all other children. They are just as smart and intelligent. They can learn. Our children are equal to other children. In developing countries, we accept that children have difficult lives and only money and support can help them build to be something better. My teaching experience in India was more positive than in my district here on Long Island. Drug abuse, corruption, and unachievable goals have been placed on my students and me. . . . My students' future isn't rosy. They live very dangerous lives. They only have a few years until they are gobbled up by a gang or something else that wants to take them. I need to provide them with skills, and I need to nourish their souls because they deserve it, and because something in them could strengthen and could survive.[41]

NOTES

1. The quotation from James Baldwin, 1961, is cited in Carol Kelly-Gangi, ed., *The Essential Wisdom of the World's Greatest Thinkers* (New York: Fall River Press, 2016), 107.
2. Dale D. Johnson, Bonnie Johnson, Stephen J. Farenga, and Daniel Ness, *Stop High-Stakes Testing* (Lanham, MD: Rowman & Littlefield, 2008), 61.
3. Ibid., 36–37.
4. Ibid., 116.
5. Tamar Lewin, "Up from the Holler: Living in Two Worlds, at Home in Neither," in *Class Matters*, eds. correspondents of the *New York Times* (New York: Times Books, 2005), 65, 66.
6. According to Merriam-Webster, *food insecure* was first used in 1977. For a complete definition and examples, see www.merriam-webster.com/dictionary/food%20insecurity.
7. The U.S. Department of Agriculture, Economic Research Service, "Definitions of Food Security," accessed July 11, 2020, www.ers.usda.gov/topics/food-nutrition-assistance/food-security-in-the-us/definitions-of-food-security.aspx.
8. Ibid.
9. The author was the third-grade teacher who later explained to the adult that such information should be kept private.
10. William Moreau and Jessamine Pilcher, "The Incentives Behind Lunch Shaming," American Bar Association, July 14, 2020, www.americanbar.org/groups/young_lawyers/publications/tyl/topics/access-to-education/incentives-behind-lunch-shaming.
11. Christina Zdanowicz, "Students' Meals Were Thrown Away over a Lunch Debt. People Donated More Than $22,000 to Pay It Off," November 19, 2019, www.cnn.com/2019/11/19/us/school-lunch-debt-donations-trnd/index.html.
12. Michelle Lou, "75% of US School Districts Report Student Meal Debt. Here's What They're Doing to Combat the Problem," May 17, 2019, www.cnn.com/2019/05/17/us/unpaid-school-lunch-debt-trnd/index.html.
13. Amir Vera, "Pennsylvania School District Tells Parents to Pay Their Lunch Debt, or Their Kids Will Go into Foster Care," July 20, 2019, www.cnn.com/2019/07/20/us/pennsylvania-school-lunch-debt-trnd/index.html.
14. The Emerson quotation is from 1860, cited in Gorton Carruth and Eugene Ehrlich, *American Quotations* (New York: Wings Books, 1988), 451.
15. Caitlin Stehling and Robert A. Mangione, "Pediatric Medical Conditions Associated with Poverty," in *Inequalities in the Early Years*, eds. Bonnie Johnson and Yvonne Pratt-Johnson (New York: Routledge, 2018), 43–56.
16. Michael Harrington, *The Other America: Poverty in the United States* (New York: Simon & Schuster, 1993), 2.
17. According to Merriam-Webster, *food desert* was first used in 1988. For additional information on the entry, see www.merriam-webster.com/dictionary/fooddesert.
18. Paula Dutko, Michele Ver Ploeg, and Tracey Farrigan, "Characteristics and Influential Factors of Food Deserts," U.S. Department of Agriculture, Economic Research report no. 140, August 2012, www.ers.usda.gov/webdocs/publications/45014/30940_err140.pdf.
19. Ibid., iii.
20. Kenzi Abou-Sabe, Christine Romo, Cynthia McFadden, and Jaimie Longoria, "COVID-19 Crisis Heaps Pressure on Nation's Food Banks," *NBC News*, July 14, 2020, www.nbcnews.com/news/us-news/covid-19-crisis-heaps-pressure-nation-s-food-banks-n1178731.
21. Laura Reiley, "Kids Go Hungry This Summer with School Lunch Programs in Peril," *Washington Post*, June 24, 2020, www.washingtonpost.com/business/2020/06/04/kids-could-go-hungry-this-summer-with-school-lunch-programs-peril.
22. Robert Klemko, "As Coronavirus Took Jobs or Workers Fell Ill, Teen Children Have Toiled Fulltime, Becoming Lifelines," *Washington Post*, June 3, 2020, www.washingtonpost.com/national/coronavirus-teens-working/2020/06/03/ff689b28-9c73-11ea-ad09-8da7ec214672_story.html.

23. Amy Finnegan, "Unemployment: How It Effects Family Behavioral Health," Center for Child and Family Policy, July 2015, http://purdue.edu/hhs/hdfs/fii/wp-content/uploads/2015/07/s_ncfis08c03.pdf.

24. Thomas J. Cottle, *Hardest Times: The Trauma of Long-Term Unemployment* (Boston: University of Massachusetts Press, 2001), 19–20.

25. Ibid.

26. Bonnie Johnson and Yvonne Pratt-Johnson, "Technology: Factors Behind the Digital Divide," in *Inequalities in the Early Years*, eds. Bonnie Johnson and Yvonne Pratt-Johnson (New York: Routledge, 2018), 1–12.

27. Brooke Auxier and Monica Anderson, "As Schools Close Due to the Coronavirus, Some U.S. Students Face a Digital 'Homework Gap,'" Pew Research Center, March 16, 2020, www.pewresearch.org/fact-tank/2020/03/16/as-schools-close-due-to-the- coronavirus-some-u-s-students-face-a-digital-homework-gap.

28. Christina Maxouris and Alice Yu, "The Coronavirus Crisis Spotlights the Inequalities in American Education," *CNN US*, April 17, 2020, www.cnn.com/2020/04/17/us/coronavirus-education-distance-learning-challenges/index.html.

29. Ibid.

30. Sites at Penn State (Education/powered by WordPress), "The Price of Standardized Testing," Penn State Sites, February 7, 2019, https://sites.psu.edu/tota19edu/2019/02/07/the-price-of-standardized-testing.

31. Scott Litin, "Factors Affecting Learning," in *Mayo Clinic Family Health Book*, 4th ed., ed. Scott Litin (Rochester, MN: Mayo Foundation for Medical Education and Research; Time Inc., 2009), 179.

32. Dale D. Johnson, Bonnie Johnson, Stephen J. Farenga, and Daniel Ness, *Trivializing Teacher Education: The Accreditation Squeeze* (Lanham, MD: Rowman & Littlefield, 2005), 114.

33. Children's Defense Fund, "Child Poverty," accessed July 16, 2020, www.childrensdefense.org/policy-priorities/child-poverty.

34. The Margaret Mead quotation is cited in Kelly-Gangi, *The Essential Wisdom*, 123.

35. U.S. Department of Education, "Promise Neighborhoods," accessed July 22, 2020, www2.ed.gov/programs/promiseneighborhoods/resources.html.

36. David L. Kirp, "How to Fix the Country's Failing Schools. And How Not To," *New York Times,* January 9, 2016, www.nytimes.com/2016/01/10/opinion/sunday/how-to-fix-the-countrys-failing-schools-and-how-not-to.html.

37. Liza Frenette, "Poverty Infiltrates Growing Number of Families," *NYSUT United*, January/February 2020, 10.

38. *Press Times*, "Back to School Store Provides School Supplies to Children in Need," July 26, 2019, 7.

39. Frenette, "Poverty Infiltrates Growing Number of Families," 10.

40. Ibid.

41. The Long Island teacher was a graduate student in a class taught by Dale D. Johnson and was an acquaintance of the author.

Bibliography

Abou-Sabe, Kenzi, Christine Romo, Cynthia McFadden, and Jaimie Longoria. "COVID-19 Crisis Heaps Pressure on Nation's Food Banks." *NBC News*, April 8, 2020. www.nbcnews.com/news/us-news/covid-19-crisis-heaps-pressure-nation-s-food-banks-n1178731.

Aitchison, Jean. *Words in the Mind: An Introduction to the Mental Lexicon,* 2nd ed. Oxford, UK: Blackwell, 1994.

American Association of Colleges for Teacher Education. "New Assessment for Teacher Candidates Rolls Out after Two Years of Field Testing: edTPA Helps Determine Whether Aspiring Teachers are [sic] Ready to Teach from Day One." November 8, 2013. https://aacte.org/2013/11/new-assessment-for-teacher-candidates-rolls-out-after-two-years-of-field-testing.

American Society of Civil Engineers. "Policy Statement 452—Investing in America's Schools." Adopted by the Board of Direction on July 13, 2018. www.asce.org/issues-and-advocacy/public-policy/policy-statement-452-investing-in-america-s-schools.

Apple, Michael. Foreword. In Dale D. Johnson, Bonnie Johnson, Stephen J. Farenga, and Daniel Ness, *Trivializing Teacher Education: The Accreditation Squeeze*, xiii. Lanham, MD: Rowman & Littlefield, 2005.

Associated Press in Washington. "US Teachers Are Not Nearly as Diverse as Their Students, New Studies Say." *The Guardian*, May 5, 2014. www.theguardian.com/world/2014/may/05/us-teachers-diverse-students-new-studies.

Auxier, Brooke, and Monica Anderson. "As Schools Close Due to the Coronavirus, Some U.S. Students Face a Digital 'Homework Gap.'" Pew Research Center, March 16, 2020. www.pewresearch.org/fact-tank/2020/03/16/as-schools-close-due-to-the-coronavirus-some-u-s-students-face-a-digital-homework-gap.

Ayres, Alex, ed. *The Wit and Wisdom of Harry S Truman.* New York: Meridian, 1998.

Bartanen, Brendan, Jason A. Grissom, Ela Joshi, and Marc M. Meredith. "Mapping Inequalities in Local Political Representation: Evidence from Ohio School Boards." *AERA Open* 4, no. 4 (December 14, 2018): 1–33. https://journals.sagepub.com/doi/full/10.1177/2332858418818074.

Bettmann, Otto L. *The Good Old Days—They Were Terrible!* New York: Random House, 1974.

Blair, Julie. "Iowa Approves Performance Pay for Its Teachers." *Education Week,* May 16, 2001.

Bowie, Liz. "8 Baltimore City Schools Closed Monday as New Heat, Facility Problems Develop after Weekend Repairs." *Baltimore Sun*, January 8, 2018. www.baltimoresun.com/news/maryland/education/bs-md-ci-city-school-closures-20180108-story.html.

Bibliography

Camera, Lauren. "Sharp Nationwide Enrollment Drop in Teacher Prep Programs Cause for Alarm." *U.S. News & World Report,* December 3, 2019. www.usnews.com/news/education-news/articles/2019-12-03/sharp-nationwide-enrollment-drop-in-teacher-prep-programs-cause-for-alarm.

Carruth, Gorton. *What Happened When.* New York: Penguin, 1989.

Carruth, Gorton, and Eugene Ehrlich. *American Quotations.* New York: Wings, 1988.

CBS Austin. "Multiple Austin-Area Schools Earn Failing Grades from Texas Education Agency." August 15, 2019. https://cbsaustin.com/local/multiple-autin-area-schools-earn-failing-grade-from-texas-education-agency.

Children's Defense Fund. "Child Poverty." Accessed July 16, 2020. www.childrensdefense.org/policy-priorities/child-poverty.

Clark, Eve. *The Lexicon in Acquisition.* Cambridge, UK: Cambridge University Press, 1993.

Cohen, Rachel. "Public School Buildings Are Falling Apart, and Students Are Suffering for It." *Washington Post,* January 8, 2018. www.washingtonpost.com/news/posteverything/wp/2018/01/08/public-school-buildings-are-falling-apart-and-students-are-suffering/for-it.

Cottle, Thomas J. *Hardest Times: The Trauma of Long-Term Unemployment.* Boston: University of Massachusetts Press, 2001.

"CPSB Receives Check for Outstanding Student Test Performance." *Guardian-Journal,* January 23, 2020.

Crain, Tricia Powell. "76 Alabama Schools on 'Failing' List." Updated January 23, 2019. www.al.com.

DeRoos, Dan. "Report Cards Are out for Ohio Schools and 309 Failed." *Cleveland 19,* September 13, 2018. http://cleveland19.com/2018/09/13/report-cards-are-out-ohio-schools-failed.

Dick, Everett. *The Sod-House Frontier:1854-1890.* Lincoln, NE: Johnsen Publishing Company, 1954.

Dutko, Paula, Michele Ver Ploeg, and Tracey Farrigan. "Characteristics and Influential Factors of Food Deserts." U.S. Department of Agriculture, Economic Research report no. 140, August 2012. www.ers.usda.gov/webdocs/publications/45014/30940_err140.pdf.

Edison, Thomas. "'To invent, you need a good imagination and a pile of junk.'" Smithsonian Libraries, February 11, 2011. http://blog.library.si.edu/blog/2011/02/11/to-invent-you-need-a-good-imagination-and-a-pile-of-junk.

edTPA. "About edTPA." Accessed May 26, 2020. www.edtpa.com/PageView.aspx?f=GEN_AboutEdTPA.html.

Eisenhower Presidential Library. "Quotes." Accessed April 17, 2020. http://eisenhowerlibrary.gov/eisenhowers/quotes.

Espelage, Dorothy, and Linda Reddy. "A Silent National Crisis: Violence Against Teachers." American Psychological Association, January 2016. http://apa.org/education/k12/teacher-victimization.

Farenga, Stephen J., Daniel Ness, Bonnie Johnson, and Dale D. Johnson. *The Importance of Average.* Lanham, MD: Rowman & Littlefield, 2010.

Faust, Drew Gilpin. *Mothers of Invention: Women of the Slaveholding South in the American Civil War.* Chapel Hill: The University of North Carolina Press, 1996.

Finnegan, Amy. "Unemployment: How it Effects Family Behavioral Health." Center for Child and Family Policy, July 2015. http://purdue.edu/hhs/hdfs/fii/wp-content/uploads/2015/07/s_ncfis08c03.pdf.

Frenette, Liza. "Poverty Infiltrates Growing Number of Families." *NYSUT United,* January/February 2020.

Gardner, Howard. "Beyond the Herd Mentality: The Minds That We Truly Need in the Future." *Education Week,* September 14, 2005.

Good, Thomas L., and Jere E. Brophy. *Looking in Classrooms,* 9th ed. New York: Pearson, 2003.

Hall, April. "Beyond the Noise." *Reading Today,* November/December 2014.

Hall, Tajma. "Report Finds Bloomer High School Needs Millions in Repairs." June 25, 2019. www.weau.com/content/news/Report-finds-Bloomer-High-School-in-need-of-millions-in-repairs-511803512.html.

Harrington, Michael. *The Other America: Poverty in the United States*. New York: Simon & Schuster, 1993.

Harris, Bracey. "Financial Support for Public Schools—and Population—Are Shrinking in Mississippi. Is There an Easy Fix?" *Clarion Ledger*, February 26, 2019. www.mississippitoday.org/2019/02/26/financial-support-for-public-schools-and-population-are-shrinking-in-mississippi-is-there-an-easy-fix.

Herring, Susan T. "Governor's Resource Team Impressed by Redbud's Beauty." *Guardian-Journal*, October 19, 2000.

———. "Stachybotrys Fungus Found at Redbud Memorial Hospital Has Been Removed." *Guardian-Journal*, December 7, 2000.

"High-Stakes Testing Tips." *Town Talk*, March 11, 2006. www.thetowntalk.com.

Hong, Barbara S. S. "Seduction of 'East Asian' Schools." In *Alternatives to Privatizing Public Education*, edited by Daniel Ness and Stephen J. Farenga, 189–198. New York: Routledge, 2017.

Ingram, Jay. *Talk, Talk, Talk: An Investigation into the Mystery of Speech*. Toronto, ON: Penguin, 1992.

Jackson, Philip W. *Life in Classrooms*. New York: Teachers College Press, 1990.

Johnson, Bonnie. "Every Day She Drunk or Gone." In *Alternatives to Privatizing Public Education and Curriculum: A Festschrift in Honor of Dale D. Johnson*, edited by Daniel Ness and Stephen J. Farenga, 169–188. New York: Routledge, 2017.

———. *Wordworks: Exploring Language Play*. Golden, CO: Fulcrum Resources, 1999.

Johnson, Bonnie, and Yvonne Pratt-Johnson. "Early Literacy: Home, School, Neighborhood." In *What's Hot in Literacy: Exemplar Models of Effective Practice*, edited by Evan Ortlieb, Stephanie Grote-Garcia, Jack Cassidy, and Earl H. Cheek Jr., 33–50. Bingley, UK: Emerald Publishing, 2020.

———. "Technology: Factors Behind the Digital Divide." In *Inequalities in the Early Years*, edited by Bonnie Johnson and Yvonne Pratt-Johnson, 1–12. New York: Routledge, 2018.

Johnson, Dale D., and Bonnie Johnson. *High Stakes: Poverty, Testing, and Failure in American Schools*, 2nd ed. Lanham, MD: Rowman & Littlefield, 2006.

Johnson, Dale D., Bonnie Johnson, Stephen J. Farenga, and Daniel Ness. *Stop High-Stakes Testing*. Lanham, MD: Rowman & Littlefield, 2008.

———. *Trivializing Teacher Education: The Accreditation Squeeze*. Lanham, MD: Rowman & Littlefield, 2005.

Katz, Michael B. *Class, Bureaucracy, & Schools: The Illusion of Educational Change in America*. New York: Praeger, 1971.

Kelly-Gangi, Carol, ed. *The Essential Wisdom of the World's Greatest Thinkers*. New York: Fall River Press, 2016.

Kercheval, Hoppy. "Failing Grades for Many WV Public Schools." *West Virginia Metro News*, September 14, 2018. http://wvmetronews.com/2018/09/14/lousy-grades-for-wv-pubic-schools.

Kirp, David L. "How to Fix the Country's Failing Schools. And How Not To." *New York Times*, January 9, 2016. www.nytimes.com/2016/01/10/opinion/sunday/how-to-fix-the-countrys-failing-schools-and-how-not-to.html.

Klemko, Robert. "As Coronavirus Took Jobs or Workers Fell Ill, Teen Children Have Toiled Fulltime, Becoming Lifelines." *Washington Post*, June 3, 2020. www.washingtonpost.com/national/coronavirus-teens-working/2020/06/03/ff689b28-9c73-11ea-ad09-8da7ec214672_story.html.

Kotler, Philip, and Gary Armstrong. *Principles of Marketing*, 7th ed. Englewood Cliffs, NJ: Prentice Hall, 1996.

Labaree, David F. *The Trouble with Ed Schools*. New Haven, CT: Yale University Press, 2004.

Levin, Claudia (Producer, Director), Meg Pinto (Associate Producer, Scriptwriter), Charles Scott (Editor), Stephen McCarthy (Cinematographer), and Allen Moore (Cinematographer). *Only a Teacher* [Television Series/Video]. Accessed May 28, 2020. http://pbs.org/onlya-teacher.

Lewin, Tamar. "Up from the Holler: Living in Two Worlds, at Home in Neither." In *Class Matters*, edited by correspondents of the *New York Times*, 65–66. New York: Times Books, 2005.

Lewis, Tristan. "Low-Performing Idaho Schools Try to Improve and Turnaround." *Local News 8*, August 22, 2018. https://localnews8.com/news/2018/08/22/low-performing-idaho-schools-try-to-improve-and-turnaround.

Litin, Scott. "Factors Affecting Learning." In *Mayo Clinic Family Health Book*, 4th ed., edited by Scott Litin, 179. Rochester, MN: Mayo Foundation for Medical Education and Research; Time Inc., 2009.

Longaberger, Dave. *Longaberger: An American Success Story*. New York: HarperBusiness, 2001.

Lou, Michelle. "75% of US School Districts Report Student Meal Debt. Here's What They're Doing to Combat the Problem." *CNN US*, May 17, 2019. www.cnn.com/2019/05/17/us/unpaid-school-lunch-debt-trnd/index.html.

Louisiana Department of Education. *Louisiana Statewide Norm-Referenced Testing Program: 2001 Test Administration Manual Grade 3: Iowa Tests of Basic Skills Form M*. Itasca, IL: Riverside.

———. *Reaching for Results: LEAP 21, Grade 4*. Baton Rouge: Louisiana Department of Education, 2001.

———. *School Analysis Model (SAM)*. Baton Rouge: Louisiana Department of Education, 2005. www.doe.state.la.us/lde/ssaa/1591.html.

Madaus, George F. "The Influence of Testing on the Curriculum." In *Issues in Curriculum: A Selection of Chapters from Past NSSE Yearbooks*, edited by Margaret J. Early and Kenneth J. Rehage, 73–111. Chicago: The National Society for the Study of Education, 1999.

Madeloni, Barbara, and Julie Gorlewski. "Radical Imagination, Not Standardization: Critical Teacher Education and the edTPA." *Teachers College Record*, June 21, 2013. www.tcrecord.org/PrintContent.asp?ContentID=17163.

Maxouris, Christina, and Alice Yu. "The Coronavirus Crisis Spotlights the Inequalities in American Education." *CNN US*, April 17, 2020. www.cnn.com/2020/04/17/us/coronavirus-education-distance-learning-challenges/index.html.

McArdle, Elaine. "What Happened to the Common Core?" *Harvard Ed. Magazine*, Fall 2014. www.gse.harvard.edu/news/ed/14/09/what-happened-common-core.

McCullough, David. *The Wright Brothers*. New York: Simon & Schuster, 2015.

McDowell, Marta. *The World of Laura Ingalls Wilder: The Frontier Landscapes that Inspired the Little House Books*. Portland, OR: Timber Press, 2017.

McGrath, Darryl. "The Big Chill: Flawed Certification and Attacks on Public Education Cause Fewer Students to Choose Teaching as Profession. Unions Push for Solutions." *NYSUT United* 6, no. 1 (Fall 2015): 20.

Menand, Louis. *The Metaphysical Club: A Story of Ideas in America*. New York: Farrar, Straus, and Giroux, 2001.

Mills, Shamane. "Why Are Fewer Wisconsin Students Studying to Become Teachers?" *WPR News*, February 5, 2019. www.wpr.org/why-are/fewer/wisconsin-students-studying-become-teachers.

Moffitt, Mike. "27 SF Unified Schools 'Low Performing,' Need Improvement, State Says: Nine Are among the Worst in the State." *San Francisco Chronicle*, February 15, 2019. www.sfchronicle.com/education/article/27-SF-Unified-schools-low-performing-education-13611519.php.

Moore, Annie E., Jean Betzner, and Mary Lewis. *The Classroom Teacher*, vol. 3. Chicago: The Classroom Teacher Inc., 1927–1928.

Moreau, William, and Jessamine Pilcher. "The Incentives Behind Lunch Shaming." American Bar Association. Accessed July 14, 2020. www.americanbar.org/groups/young_lawyers/publications/tyl/topics/access-to-education/incentives-behind-lunch-shaming.

Morgan, Sarah. *Sarah Morgan: The Civil War Diary of a Southern Woman*. Edited by Charles East. New York: Simon & Schuster, 1991.

National Aeronautics and Space Administration. "Welcome to the Beginner's Guide to Kites." Accessed June 2, 2020. http://grc.nasa.gov/www/K-12/airplane/shortk.html.

National Center for Education Statistics. "School Crime." Accessed May 17, 2020. https://nces.ed.gov/fastfacts/display.asp?id=49.
National Commission on Excellence in Education. *A Nation at Risk: The Imperative for Educational Reform*. Washington, DC: US Government Printing Office, 1983. Accessed April 20, 2020. https://ww2.ed.gov/pubs/NatAtRisk/members.html.
National Museum of American History. "Industry and Manufacturing." Accessed March 2, 2020. https://americanhistory.si.edu/collections/subjects/industry-manufacturing.
Neira, Maria. "We Can Learn from What Finland Is NOT Doing." *New York State United Teachers*, October 2012.
The Nobel Prize. "Edwin G. Krebs." 1992. http://nobelprize.org/prizes/medicine/1992/krebs/biographical.
———. "F. Sherwood Rowland." Accessed May 31, 2020. http://nobelprize.org/prizes/chemistry/1995/Rowland/biographical.
NPR. "The Teachers' Revolt." *THE WEEK*, June 1, 2018.
O'Brien, E. "Teachers Get Locked Down but Paid Up: Educators Bust Out of Schools for Better Pay." *News-Star*, January 29, 2001, 1.
PBS News Hour. "Oklahoma Teachers Are Posting Their Crumbling Textbooks Online." April 3, 2018. www.pbs.org/newshour/nation/oklahoma-teachers-are-posting-their-crumbling-textbooks-online.
Penn State, sites at (Education/powered by WordPress). "The Price of Standardized Testing." Penn State Sites, February 7, 2019. https://sites.psu.edu/tota19edu/2019/02/07/the-price-of-standardized-testing.
Pfanz, Donald. *Clara Barton's Civil War*. Yardley, PA: Westholme Publishing, 2018.
Pinker, Steven. *The Language Instinct: How the Mind Creates Language*. New York: Harper-Perennial, 1994.
Press Times. "Back to School Store Provides School Supplies to Children in Need." July 26, 2019.
Race to the Top Fund. "Program Description." Accessed June 2, 2020. www2.ed.gov/programs/racetothetop/index.html.
Rank, Mark Robert. *One Nation, Underprivileged: Why American Poverty Affects Us All*. New York: Oxford University Press, 2006.
Reich, Robert B. "Standards for What?" *Education Week*, June 20, 2001, 64.
Reiley, Laura. "Kids Go Hungry This Summer with School Lunch Programs in Peril." *Washington Post*, June 4, 2020. www.washingtonpost.com/business/2020/06/04/kids-could-go-hungry-this-summer-school-lunch-programs-peril.
Reilly, Katie. "The Life of the American Teacher." *TIME*, September 24, 2018.
Riggs, Liz. "Why Do Teachers Quit?" *The Atlantic*, October 24, 2013. www.theatlantic.com/education/print/2013/10/why-do-teachers-quit/280699.
Robbins, Alexandra. "Teacher Deserve More Respect." *New York Times*, March 22, 2020.
Rodriguez, Mariana. "Rockford Public Schools Get Failing Grade from the State of Illinois." MyStateLine.com, October 31, 2018. www.mystateline.com/news/rockford-public-schools-get-failing-grade-from-the-state-of-illinois.
Ryan, Mackenzie. "State: 341 Iowa Schools Are Struggling and Need Comprehensive or Targeted Improvements." *Des Moines Register*, December 18, 2018. www.desmoinesregister.com/story/news/education/2018/12/18/iowa-school-report-card-performance-profiles-every-student-succeeds-act-nclb-needs-improvement/2317321002.
Sarjala, Jukka. "Equality and Cooperation: Finland's Path to Excellence." *American Educator* 37, no. 1 (Spring 2013): 32–36.
Sedgwick, Josephine. "25-Year-Old Textbooks and Holes in the Ceiling: Inside America's Public Schools." *New York Times*, April 16, 2018. www.nytimes.com/2018/04/16/reader-center/us-public-schools-conditions.html.
Skolnick, Jerome H., and Elliott Currie. *Crisis in American Institutions*, 11th ed. Boston: Allyn and Bacon, 2000.
Smith, Kara. "Southern Tier Educators Brainstorm Teacher Shortage Solutions." *NYSUT United*, May/June 2020.

Souto-Manning, Mariana. "The Teaching Profession Provides Little Room for Growth." *New York Times*, September 11, 2014. http://nytimes.com/roomfordebate/2014/09/11/how-to-diversify-teaching/the-teaching-profession-provides-little-room-for-growth.

Stehling, Caitlin, and Robert A. Mangione. "Pediatric Medical Conditions Associated with Poverty." In *Inequalities in the Early Years*, edited by Bonnie Johnson and Yvonne Pratt-Johnson, 43–56. New York: Routledge, 2018.

Strauss, Valerie. "Teacher Slams Scripted Common Core Lessons That Must Be Taught 'Word for Word.'" *Washington Post*, November 30, 2013. www.washingtonpost.com/news/answer-sheet/wp/2013/11/30/teacher-slams-scripted-common-core-lessons-that-must-be-taught-word-for-word.

Taketa, Kristen. "See if California Has Identified Your School as Low-Performing." *San Diego Union-Tribune*, February 5, 2019. http://sandiegouniontribune.com/news/education/sd-me-worst-performing-schools-20190204-story.html.

"The Marshall Plan, Speech by US Secretary of State George C. Marshall," June 5, 1947, History and Public Policy Program Digital Archive, Congressional Record. http://digitalarchive.wilsoncenter.org/document/116183.

THE WEEK. "Only in America." August 17/24, 2018.

Thomas Jr., Robert. "David Longaberger, Basket Maker, Dies at 64." *New York Times*, March 22, 1999. www.nytimes.com/1999/03/22/us/david-longaberger-basket-maker-dies-at-64.html.

Thompson, Anne Bahr. "Brand Positioning and Brand Creation." In *Brands and Branding*, edited by Rita Clifton and John Simmons, 79–95. Princeton, NJ: Bloomberg Press, 2003.

Tornay, Kaylee. "Teachers, Parents Report Increase in Unruly Students." *Associated Press*, June 19, 2018. www.apnews.com/235024be3f984493b54aec8bfbdd2d4c.

Truong, Debbie. "'Borderline Criminal': Many Public Schools Teeter on the Edge of Decrepitude." *Washington Post*, May 25, 2019. http://washingtonpost.com/local/education/borderline-criminal-thats-the-condition-of-decrepit-public-schools/2019/05/25/bad60064-556f-11e9-814f-e2f46.

University of California, Los Angeles. "State Normal School Opens in Los Angeles." Accessed April 21, 2020. https://alumni.gseis.ucla.edu/?timeline=state-normal-school-opens-in-los-angeles.

University of Northern Iowa. "History and Traditions." Accessed April 21, 2020. https://uni.edu/resources/history-traditions.

U.S. Department of Agriculture, Economic Research Service. "Definitions of Food Security." Accessed July 11, 2020. www.ers.usda.gov/topics/food-nutrition-assistance/food-security-in-the-us/definitions-of-food-security.aspx.

U.S. Department of Education. "Every Student Succeeds Act (ESSA)." Accessed June 21, 2021. http://ed.gov/essa?src=rn.

———. "Promise Neighborhoods." Accessed July 22, 2020. www2.ed.gov/programs/promiseneighborhoods/resources.html.

U.S. House of Representatives. "National Defense Education Act." https://history.house.gov/Records-and-Research/Listing/lfp_006.

Vera, Amir. "Pennsylvania School District Tells Parents to Pay Their Lunch Debt, or Their Kids Will Go into Foster Care." *CNN US*, July 21, 2019. www.cnn.com/2019/07/20/us/pennsylvania-school-lunch-debt-trnd/index.html.

Wallman, Brittany. "Public Schools Get Failing Grades in New Survey by Fort Lauderdale Residents." *South Florida Sun Sentinel*, June 8, 2019. www.sun-sentinel.com/local/broward/fort-lauderdale/fl-ne-fort-lauderdale-schools-20190608poilgxp6nvbyrgxcb72vbevnny-story.html.

Wexler, Natalie. "The Radical Case for Teaching Kids Stuff." *The Atlantic* 324, no. 2 (August 2019).

Whelan, Sister Ellen. *The Sisters' Story: Saint Marys Hospital—Mayo Clinic 1889–1939*. Rochester, MN: Mayo Foundation for Medical Education and Research, 2002.

Zdanowicz, Christina. "Students' Meals Were Thrown Away over a Lunch Debt. People Donated More Than $22,000 to Pay It Off." *CNN US*, November 28, 2019. www.cnn.com/2019/11/19/us/school-lunch-debt-donations-trnd/index.html.

Index

Aitchison, Jean, 91n3
American Association of Colleges for Teacher Education (AACTE), 121–122
American Bar Association (ABA), 137
American Federation of Teachers, 141
American Society of Civil Engineers, 10–11
Apple, Michael, 114–115

Back to School Store, 141
Baldwin, James, 135
Barton, Clara, 108
"best teachers," 9
Bettmann, Otto L., 109, 129n1
Blair, Julie, 99
Born, Max, 128
Buttimer, Chris, 117

Camera, Lauren, 131n56
Children's Defense Fund, 140
Clark, Eve, 79
Common Core State Standards (CCSS), 114, 115–116, 117
Common Schools, 107
Cottle, Thomas J., 139
Council for the Accreditation of Educator Preparation (CAEP), 123
COVID-19, 120, 128, 138, 139
curricular decisions, 124–129

Dewey, John, 109

Dick, Everett, 108, 109, 124
Duckworth, Eleanor, 117
Duke, Bryan, 122
Dutko, Paula; Ver Ploeg, Michele; & Farrigan, Tracey, 138

East, Charles, 131n48
Edison, Thomas A., 128
edTPA, 121
Eisenhower, Dwight D., 103, 110
Emerson, Ralph Waldo, 137
Every Student Succeeds Act (ESSA), 118

failing schools: branding, 5; headlines, 7; recipe for, 5
Farenga, Stephen J.; Ness, Daniel; Johnson, Bonnie; & Johnson, Dale D., 128
Faust, Drew Gilpin, 119
Firth, J. R., 6
food desert, 138
food insecure, 136–137
Frenette, Liza, 141, 143n37

Gardner, Howard, 12
Good, Thomas L., & Brophy, Jere E., 132n61
Gray, LaRuth, 121

Hall, April, 115–116
Harrington, Michael, 138

Ingram, Jay, 91n3
insufficient school funding, 9–10
international comparisons, 11–12

Jackson, Philip W., 122, 126–127
Johnson, Bonnie, 14n20, 114
Johnson, Bonnie, & Pratt-Johnson, Yvonne, 118–119, 131n35, 139
Johnson, Dale D., & Johnson, Bonnie, 113
Johnson, Dale D.; Johnson, Bonnie; Farenga, Stephen J.; & Ness, Daniel, 116–117, 123, 135–136, 140

Katz, Michael B., 5, 107, 126
Kirp, David L., 143n36
Klemko, Robert, 142n22
Krebs, Edwin G., 127

Labaree, David F., 120
Levin, Claudia, 129n3
Lewin, Tamar, 142n5
Longaberger, David, 126
lunch shaming, 137

Madaus, George F., 129
Madeloni, Barbara, & Gorlewski, Julie, 123
Mayo Clinic Family Health Book, 140
McArdle, Elaine, 131n38
McCullough, David, 127
McGrath, Darryl, 132n63
Mead, Margaret, 140
Menand, Louis, 109

A Nation at Risk, 6, 111
National Aeronautics and Space Administration (NASA), 128–129
National Center for Education Statistics, 120
National Commission on Excellence in Education, 111–112, 113
National Defense Education Act, 110
Neira, Maria, 11
New York State United Teachers, 141
No Child Left Behind (NCLB), Public Law 107-110, 113
normal schools, 108

Pinker, Steven, 91n3

poverty: complexities of, 15–16, 64–65; costs of, 95, 139
Promise Neighborhoods, 140
public schools, unreasonable expectations, 8–9

Race to the Top, 117–118
Redbud Elementary, the pupils, offenses committed as adults, 3
Redbud Elementary, the school today, 4
Redbud Elementary twenty years ago: afterschool meetings, 25–26, 27–28, 30, 32, 33–34, 37, 45–46, 85; art classes, 67–68; assistant principal, 25, 58; book fair, 50; the building, 17–18, 35, 58, 59, 60, 61–62, 64, 76, 88–89; classroom supplies, 18–19, 38, 40, 44, 80, 86–87, 88; demonstration lessons, 36; dress code review, 87–88; Dr. Martin Luther King Jr., 33, 63; Drug Awareness Week, 43, 49; health problems, 24, 26, 29, 30, 31, 32, 47, 59, 84, 88, 98; honors day, 100; Ku Klux Klan, 36; lack of playground equipment, 17, 41; lesson plans, 27–28, 29, 57, 68, 81; meeting the teachers, 19–20; money spent on testing, 86; the neighborhood, 21, 28, 36, 66, 87; parents/guardians, 26, 27, 29, 32, 33, 41, 50, 51, 52, 62, 63, 69–70, 73, 75, 87, 95–96; parent/teacher conferences, 38–39; politicians, 98, 99; prior knowledge, 28, 51, 63–64, 79; professional development day, 74; the pupils, 20, 29, 30, 31, 33, 36, 41, 43, 44, 50, 51, 52, 53–54, 55, 56–57, 59–60, 64, 66, 69–70, 71, 72, 79, 84–85, 87, 89, 94, 96, 99, 100; recommendations, 101–103; report cards, 33; school pictures, 35, 57; school's designation, 17, 53, 85–86; student teachers, 56, 75, 93; teacher generosity, 47, 58, 75; teacher handbook, 20–21; teachers' duties, 22, 24, 32, 39, 40, 42–43, 55, 89–90, 93, 94; teacher turnover, 17, 38, 40, 46, 104; technology, 23, 34, 37, 46, 51, 67, 76, 88; test administration, 77; test effects on pupils, 75, 80, 83, 89; test preparation, 17, 28, 37, 42, 65, 67, 72,

78, 84, 86; test-prep rallies, 71, 74; test results, 96–98; test security, 77–79, 80–81, 82, 84, 85; vandalism, 55, 57
Redbud, the town: today, 3–4; twenty years ago, 15, 43
Reich, Robert B., 104
Reiley, Laura, 142n21
Reilly, Katie, 132n69
Riggs, Liz, 14n24
Rowland, F. Sherwood, 127

Sarjala, Jukka, 11–12
school board members, characteristic of, 8
School of Academic Distinction, 65–66
Sedgwick, Josephine, 9
Skolnick, Jerome H., & Currie, Elliott, 8
Smith, Kara, 132n62
Souto-Manning, Mariana, 117
Sputnik, 110
standards, 111–112, 114

Stehling, Caitlin, & Mangione, Robert A., 138
Strauss, Valerie, 116

teacher educators, 122–123
teacher pay, recent years, 123–124
teacher shortage, 121–122
test-taking tips, 4
Tornay, Kaylee, 120
Truong, Debbie, 10

U.S. Department of Agriculture (USDA), Economic Research Service, 136–137
U.S. creativity, 12–13

western schools in the 1800s, 108–109
Wexler, Natalie, 117
Wilder, Laura Ingalls, 108
Wright, Susan Koerner; Wright, Wilbur, & Wright, Orville, 127–128

About the Author

Bonnie Johnson earned her Ph.D. at the University of Wisconsin–Madison. She currently teaches classes in the departments of Curriculum and Instruction and Education Specialties at St. John's University in New York City. Dr. Johnson was a public school classroom teacher for 14 years. She was the recipient of the University of Wisconsin–Madison's Distinguished Teacher of Teachers Award and was named an Eminent Literacy Scholar by *The e-Journal of Literacy and Social Responsibility*. Dr. Johnson is the author, coauthor, or editor of eight books, numerous book chapters, and journal articles and has coauthored more than 200 instructional texts for elementary, middle school, and adult learners. She is the co-editor of the international juried journal *The Reading Professor*. Dr. Johnson's research addresses social inequalities in the early years, the impact of poverty on vocabulary acquisition, word origins, and histories of figurative expressions.

www.ingramcontent.com/pod-product-compliance
Lightning Source LLC
Chambersburg PA
CBHW020740230426
43665CB00009B/504